BOARD GAME CAFÉ MANAGEMENT

Book of Company Rules, Contracts, SOPs, Checklists, Proposals, and more for board game café

Authored by
Ardiawan Bagus Harisa
Pulung Nurtantio Andono

TABLE OF CONTENTS

TABLE OF FIGURES

TABLE OF TABLES

PREFACE

This book is created as a comprehensive operational guide for managing a board game café, Dhadhu Board Game Café (or simply, Dhadhu Café). Over time, this book should be modified to adapt to operational developments in the field. The book is created with the aim of facilitating management and operational staff in performing their duties and minimizing errors. The content in this book is created very briefly and clearly so that it can be implemented directly in the field. Finally, please note that the content provided in this book is mostly based on our experience in managing Dhadhu Café that is in South East Asia region, Republic of Indonesia. Therefore, please use this book as a reference at your own risk. The financial data provided in this book uses Indonesian currency (Rupiah; Rp) and might be augmented, synthesized, or even removed due to confidentiality reasons.

ACKNOWLEDGMENT

As the business of Dhadhu Board Game Café (PT. Nagara Kaya Karsa) progresses, we as authors and practitioners also continue to learn. We want to express appreciation to all of my current and former staff and partners. Thanks to:

1. Batch 1: Wicak, Sultan, Samirah, Ozzy, Anton, Ko Yochan, Ko Alfons, Gadis, Ama, Tegar, Icha. Albert.
2. Batch 2: Tia, Arif, Rifandi, Derry, Akbar, Elok.
3. Batch 3: Risa, Elita, Purwanti, Mikha, Ganang, Arsya, Hamim, Lintang, Putri, Salasa, Abyan, Aini, Xeni.
4. Batch 4: Tsabita, Alika, Norman, Dimas.
5. Mr. Rifki Bachtiar & family, and Mr. Rahmatullah and family.
6. Everyone who support the creation of this book.

INTRODUCTION

As we mentioned earlier, the purpose of the writing of this book is to provide you, board game café enthusiasts, with general knowledge of how to manage a board game café. So, that may be someday you are able to open your own. Once again, the contents of this book are mainly based on our field experiences. However, we are also based on several studies supporting our thinking. Please read the introduction chapter for better clarity.

What is a board game café, anyway?

A board game café is a place where people go to play board games and card games while they eat and drink. You usually have to pay to get in or rent a table, and then you can pick from a bunch of games to play (Konieczny, 2019). The staff can help you learn how to play if you don't know. Some of these cafés also sell the games they have. It seems like these cafés started in South Korea. Back in 2004, Seoul had 130 of them (Donovan, 2018).

The basic advice was to make sure your team gets trained up well, keep a handle on service quality, bring in a seasoned manager for the restaurant, and amp up your promos, like offering deals for students. To really knock it out of the park, focus on giving your crew solid training, stay on top of quality control, find a top-notch manager, and mix things up with promos that catch people's attention, especially the student crowd (Gurhananda & Wandebori, n.d.). Because of those reasons, we decide to write this book for our own company, and share with you board game enthusiasts.

Cafés have different styles, including how they look and the unique design choices made by the owners to help bring in customers. There are three main types of café styles: fashion cafés, theme cafés, and view cafés (Hou, 2013). Fashion cafés keep up with cultural trends and have stylish designs. Theme cafés are based on the interests of the owners, like music, books, or antiques. View cafés not only serve food but also have nice views, either natural or created. Each view café has its own special style and they often decorate to match the surroundings. By combining coffee and nice views, these cafés attract different kinds of customers. Overall, view cafés offer more than just coffee by giving customers a pleasant environment to enjoy, making their leisure experience better.

According to this study, using most influential parameters (capital, number of employees, scale of cafe) on the stylistic cafes, fashion café is ranked 1, followed by view café, and finally the theme café. Realizing that board game café is a theme café, please take your consideration carefully when you want to establish one. Fortunately, this book also presents documents template might be significant to consider your café's capital, employees, and scale of your café.

We hope this introduction gives you a glimpse of the importance of board game café and its management as a business potential you may want to establish.

Let's begin!

I. COMPANY PROFILE

A. ABOUT

Dhadhu Board Game Café (PT. Nagara Kaya Karsa) is a company engaged in the food and beverage industry, as well as the creative sector (Harisa, 2020). In addition to selling café-style food and drinks, we also offer services such as game-based learning/workshops, in-game marketing, and other business-to-business solutions. Our vision is to spread the spirit and benefits of board games to all layers of society. Please, visit our Instagram @dhadhucafe.id if you are interested.

Figure 1. Dhadhu Café Logo with a tosca-green and orange as main colors.

B. ORGANIZATIONAL STRUCTURE

Here is the organizational structure of Dhadhu Café:

1. **Director & Creative Director**: The Director & Creative Director oversee the overall direction and creative aspects of the café, ensuring alignment with the company's vision and objectives.
2. **Manager/Supervisor (SPV)***: The Manager/Supervisor is responsible for the day-to-day operations of the café, including staff management, customer service, and ensuring smooth functioning of all departments.
3. **Finance**: The Finance department handles financial matters such as budgeting, accounting, and financial reporting. This position may be combined with the Manager role if feasible.
4. **Marketing**: The Marketing team is tasked with promoting the café, attracting customers, and implementing marketing strategies to increase sales and brand visibility.

5. **Kitchen***: The Kitchen staff are responsible for food preparation, ensuring quality, hygiene, and timely delivery of food orders to customers.
6. **Bar***: The Bar team manages the beverage section of the café, including preparing drinks, maintaining inventory, and ensuring customer satisfaction at the bar area.
7. **Game Master**: The Game Master facilitates game-based activities, workshops, and events, ensuring an enjoyable experience for customers engaging in board games and related activities.
8. **Cashier**: The Cashier handles transactions, manages the cash register, and ensures accuracy in billing and payments.
9. **Security**: The Security personnel ensure the safety and security of the café premises, staff, and customers.

Note: The "*" symbol indicates positions that are preferably filled with full-time staff. The Finance position may be combined with the Manager role if feasible, considering workload and responsibilities. These are the essential positions. If the remaining positions are not filled by full-time staff, the associated risks are not as high as the mandatory positions.

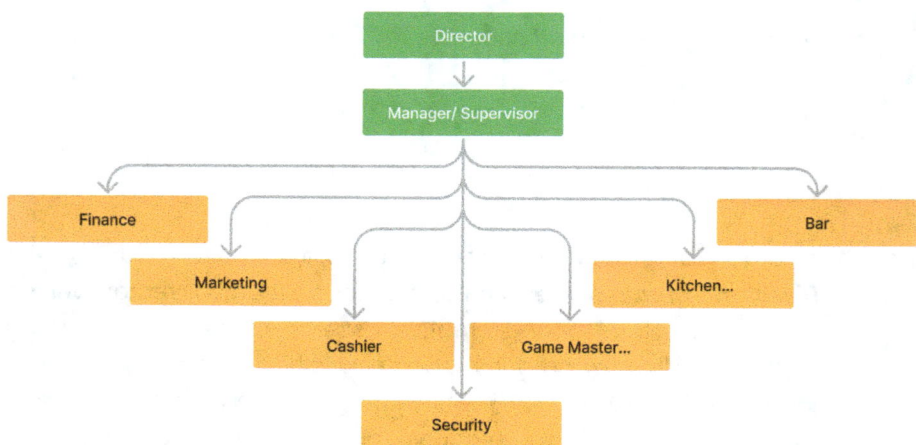

Figure 2. The organizational structure of Dhadhu Café

C. ORGANIZATIONAL CULTURES

Here are the organizational culture practices at Dhadhu Café that must be adhered to by staff:
1. Take responsibility according to your role or position.

2. Communicate effectively with each other.
3. Maintain a positive mindset and seek solutions.
4. Collaborate with the team.
5. Engage in religious practices if it aligns with your beliefs.
6. Provide excellent service to customers.
7. Maintain personal hygiene and cleanliness in the environment.

These practices contribute to fostering a positive and productive work environment at Dhadhu Café. We believe a productive team comes from a strong collective culture. Therefore, embedding a positive working culture in each individual matters.

II. BUSINESS MODEL

The Business Model is a concept that describes how a company creates products or services, delivers value to customers, sells and markets them, and understands its sources of revenue and expenses (Osterwalder & Pigneur, 2010). The business model we utilize is summarized in a document called the BMC (Business Model Canvas). Additionally, this BMC is also incorporated into a document known as a pitch deck.

A pitch deck is a presentation used by entrepreneurs or business professionals to showcase their business idea or product to potential investors or partners (Baehr & Loomis, 2015). It's a brief and visual summary of key business aspects like the problem being solved, the solution offered, target market, revenue model, competition, and growth strategy. By including the Business Model Canvas (BMC) in the pitch deck, we ensure clarity and consistency in communicating our value proposition, market position, and growth plans. This approach builds trust and confidence among stakeholders in the viability of our business model.

BUSINESS MODEL
CANVAS • COMPONENTS

Key Partners	Key Activities	Value Propositions	Customer Relationships	Customer Segments
All restaurant stuff	All restaurant needs	Playground to having fun, eating, and socializing	Semi personal-dedicated, community, & co-creation relationship	Gamers who want to play and buy
Game master and creative team for community	Community & creative team development & management, expo	Super comfy-cheap space	Board games community & forum, events, games collection	Non-gamer youth, adult, & kids, FAMILY
Suppliers & distributors	Game management		Signature menu & games	Researching students who search for references
Communities	Campaign	Exclusive games for free	**Channels**	Surrounding resident
	Key Resources		Board games community & forum	Institution, corp, tour agency, tourist
	All restaurant needs	Workshop space for public and educator	M-to-M, Socmed, website, ads, on-spot	
	Creative team: Game masters, IP developer		Dhadhu Roller App	
	Games collection			
	Apps			

Cost Structure	Revenue Streams
All restaurant needs, Game Master, game maintenance and addition, distribution, license, all creative events	Food & Beverage, Game retail, membership (for geek table), event partner, Top-up

Figure 3. Dhadhu Café's Business Model Canvas (BMC).

A component of a pitch deck or presentation that provides an overview of the competitive landscape in which a company operates is competitors analysis. It typically includes information about direct and indirect competitors, their strengths and weaknesses, market share, pricing strategies, key differentiators, and any potential threats or opportunities they present to the company. This slide helps investors and stakeholders understand the market dynamics and the company's positioning relative to its competitors. According to the figure, we can create a positive narrative, even though the positions of our café can be depicted negatively with the same figure. Here is our positive narrative: The blue circle, representing an updated analysis from the previous positioning (orange circle), illustrates that Dhadhu Café is very affordable while offering a comfortable ambiance. Furthermore, Dhadhu Café provides a variety of exclusive games for free and is strategically located.

COMPETITION
COMPETITORS

Figure 4. Competitors analysis of Dhadhu Café.

There are routine events at Dhdahu Café, including playday, tournament, workshop, and community gathering. Playday is a monthly public event where we encourage customers in our café to meet each other, even if they are strangers. Through this event, we aim to foster stronger bonds and expand our network. At the end of each month, we host a game tournament to allow our community to showcase their competitive spirit and climb the leaderboard. We frequently offer workshops, such as game-based learning for teachers and students. Despite being a board game café, our community is not limited; we are part of the Semarang City Creative Network.

EVENTS & PROGRAM
MOODBOARD

Playday

Tournament   **Academy**

Figure 5. Events in Dhadhu Café: public playday, game tournament, and skill academy

III. COMPANY RULES

A business rule sets boundaries or guidelines for how a business operates (Kardasis & Loucopoulos, 2004). It can tell us what to do in certain situations or simply whether something is true or false. These rules help shape how the business works and guide its behavior. They make sure decisions are consistent, the business follows the law, and things run smoothly, which saves time and money. Plus, they lower risks and make customers happier, providing a solid structure for growth while keeping the company's goals and values in check.

A. OBLIGATIONS/ RESPONSIBILITIES

1. Adhering to Company Rules (arriving and leaving work) punctually is mandatory:
    a. A delay of 5 minutes will result in a deduction of 1 hour from the daily wage of each staff member.
    b. Delays exceeding 1 hour (without approved permission) will be considered as absence. Repeat offenses will result in a Warning Letter.
2. Implementing 4S+1S (Smile, Greeting, Politeness, Courtesy) (Indonesian: Senyum, Salam, Sopan, Santun) with everyone, and promptly performing prayers (Salat) when due.
3. Adhering to Uniform Regulations. Wearing the designated uniform is compulsory. Dhadhu uniform shirts are to be worn at least once a week, especially on weekends.
    a. Cashiers & Game Masters: Wearing an apron while serving customers.
    b. Kitchen & Baristas: Wearing an apron during production activities.
4. Adhering to Health Protocols. Washing hands before engaging in any activity and wearing a mask when feeling unwell.
5. Maintaining Cleanliness and Orderliness in the Workplace.
    a. Maintaining and caring for café facilities. Minimum cleanliness standards must be maintained.
    b. After using the restroom, it should be wiped dry with tissue and room freshener should be sprayed once.
    c. Proper disposal of trash in designated bins if nearby areas have litter.
6. Personal Appearance and Grooming:

     a. Maintaining personal hygiene, particularly for frontliner staff who must carry spare shirts.

     b. Female staff must touch up their appearance, including applying minimal lipstick.

     c. Keeping hair and facial hair neatly groomed.

7. Observing Break and Prayer Etiquette. Taking breaks for meals and/or prayers should be done alternately with other staff and not during peak order times.

8. Attending Weekly Briefings. Briefings are held during the first 10 minutes before preparing or after closing orders.

9. Participating in Monthly General Cleaning (GC). Supervisors/Managers or Directors lead GC activities. The date is determined through discussion. Refreshments must be provided. GC can be conducted for 2 hours at the end of operating hours. Keeping Personal Belongings such as bags, jackets, and helmets neatly stored in lockers or office drawers.

10. Rotating responsibilities for cleaning the prayer room and toilets as per the schedule.

11. Requesting permission before leaving or being absent from work and taking the initiative to find a replacement:

     a. Providing evidence in case of illness.

     b. Leave requests must be submitted at least 7 days in advance. Employees must seek permission from colleagues and supervisors within their respective divisions.

Notes: No rules are created to burden staff's work; rules are made and always should be made to organize and control teamwork, thus lightening the workload of all staff.

B. PROHIBITIONS

1. Excessive use or playing of mobile phones.
2. Using raw materials for personal purposes.
3. Engaging in matters related to racial, religious, ethnic, or criminal issues.
4. Leaving the workplace without permission.
5. Engaging in prolonged conversations with acquaintances during working hours.
6. Eating or drinking while standing at the cashier counter.
7. Damaging workplace facilities for any reason.

8. Engaging in gossip, rumors, or other toxic activities.

C. IMPORTANT NOTES

1. Sanctions for violations of company rules include verbal or written warnings (in the form of warning letters). If an accumulation of warning letters exceeds 3 times, the company reserves the right to terminate the staff member's employment.
2. If a staff member wishes to leave before the contract ends, they must provide information at least 1 month in advance until management finds a replacement. Penalties apply to staff who violate this, requiring them to pay the basic salary for the remaining months as per the contract.
3. Full-time staff are entitled to annual leave of 7 days, on:
   a. January 1st (New Year) 1 day off.
   b. Eid al-Fitr 4 days off.
   c. August 16th (night of devotion) 1 day off.
   d. Religious holidays other than Islam 1 day off.
4. Staff receive facilities including:
   a. Purchase with a 25% discount for personal and family use.
   b. Coffee 500g, sugar 1kg, milk 1L, and other ingredients or cash for experiments worth Rp. 100,000 (per month).
   c. First aid kit for work accidents.
   d. Employment and health insurance (full-time staff) after working for a minimum of 1 year as per regulations.
   e. Training or certification once (full-time staff).
5. Menu experiments:
   a. Staff may conduct experiments as per point 3a in the Important Notes section and pitch them to management. There are 2 options:
   b. Royalty of 5% net profit for the menu and recipe after validation for 1 month and while the menu is sold.
   c. One-time purchase of Rp. 250,000 for drinks and snacks, and Rp. 500,000 for main courses.
6. Staff (especially full-time) are entitled to bonuses determined by the company or as per the contract. There are 2 options:
   a. According to daily targets:
      i. Daily sales above Rp. 2,000,000 → Rp. 12,000.
      ii. Daily sales above Rp. 2,500,000 → Rp. 16,000.
      iii. Daily sales above Rp. 3,000,000 → Rp. 20,000.

b. According to the percentage (%) of the number of menu items sold → 2% of net profit.
7. If there are reservations outside of operating hours, staff must adhere to those hours and continue working for a total of 8 hours. For overtime event wages ranging from Rp. 50,000 to Rp. 75,000 depending on staff status, reservation size, and type (private or regular). If it's not an event, overtime costs are according to working hours.

D. HOSPITALITY

1. Welcoming Customers:
    a. Always greet customers as they enter the café, such as "Welcome to Dhadhu, friend!"
    b. Seek permission before communicating with customers and express gratitude.
    c. Take note of customers' orders and recommend menu items.
    d. Repeat customers' orders.
    e. Seat customers and assist with table positioning.
    f. Receive and hand over items to customers using both hands if possible.
    g. Check the delivered items and what remain.
2. Reservation Procedures:
    a. Regular reservations (table): minimum of 4 customers, maximum of 20 (indoor) or 30 (outdoor), with an advance payment of Rp. 10,000 per customer made via transfer or cash. Customers must indicate their menu choices promptly.
    b. Private reservations (indoor): minimum order of Rp. 4,000,000.
    c. Private reservations (indoor & outdoor): minimum order of Rp. 6,000,000.
    d. For private reservations outside of operating hours, a staff overtime fee of Rp. 100,000 is charged.
3. Game Borrowing and Rental Procedures:
    a. Customers are charged Rp. 10,000 for game borrowing per day, unlimited quantity. Note that every game exchange must be handled by the game master.

b. For medium or heavy game mastering, reservations are required before the designated day.

c. Rental prices for games:
   i. Casual: Rp. 30,000 for 3 days.
   ii. Medium: Rp. 40,000 for 3 days.
   iii. Heavy: Rp. 50,000 for 3 days.

d. Rental procedure: Customers place orders through the game master or IG, choose game titles, and then games will be delivered via online delivery or customers can pick them up directly. Games must be returned by the designated return date. For example, if borrowed at 12 PM on the 1st, it must be returned before 12 PM on the 3rd.

4. Handling Complaints:
   a. Begin with phrases such as, "Excuse me, how can we assist you?" or "Apologies for the inconvenience, I will inquire with management for a solution."
   b. For significant errors on our part/management, offer compliments such as complimentary snacks or drinks.
   c. For customer errors, respond with phrases like, "Apologies, I have consulted with management and based on the applicable rules, therefore..., thank you for your understanding."
   d. When customers complain, always inquire about the issue and offer assistance. If unable to resolve immediately, consult with a supervisor.

5. Lost Items:
   a. Place lost items in the bottom drawer of the counter.
   b. Staff are prohibited from using lost items, and announcements are made via Instagram @dhadhucafe.id.

E. CONFLICTS

1. All minor issues that can be resolved independently by employees, please take the initiative and handle the problem in a professional manner with the help of Supervisor (SPV).

2. If there are issues that cannot be resolved independently, please discuss with the Manager, Division Coordinator, or Creative Director.

F. PAYROLL

Payroll Formula:
Salary = Base Salary (or Training) + Incentives + Daily Incentive – Deductions

1. Gross Salary:
    a. Base Salary or Training: as per contract.
    b. Daily Salary = Base Salary or Training / 26 working days.
    c. Hourly Salary = Daily Salary / 9.
2. Incentives:
    a. Purchase (Hamim; a kitchen staff) = Rp. 250,000.
    b. Sauce Making (Hamim) = Rp. 150,000.
    c. Employee of the Month (attendance punctuality > 85% and other KPIs, based on staff evaluation) = Rp. 25,000 part-time, Rp. 50,000 full-time.
    d. Staff fuel [Tentative & conditional] = Rp. 25,000.
3. Daily Incentives:
    a. Sales > Target (Rp. 2,000,000) = Rp. 12,000.
    b. Sales > Target (Rp. 2,500,000) = Rp. 16,000.
    c. Sales > Target (Rp. 3,000,000) = Rp. 20,000.
4. Deductions:
    a. Late > 5 minutes = Hourly Salary * number of late hours.
    b. Absence or day off = Daily Salary.
    c. Any outstanding debts.

IV. STANDARD OPERATIONAL PROCEDURE (SOP)

Standardization is about finding consistent solutions for common problems across different fields like science. It aims to bring order to a situation. This usually involves creating and enforcing standards. These standards are the end result of standardization efforts and in quality systems, they're documents related to quality. SOPs, or Standard Operating (or Operational) Procedures, are detailed instructions for doing a specific task consistently (Manghani, 2011). They specify who does what and when or how to carry out an activity. SOPs make sure work is done the same way every time by everyone involved. Well-written SOPs help control quality and prevent mistakes, reducing waste and rework. They need to be regularly reviewed and updated to stay effective. Without SOPs, maintaining quality systems becomes difficult.

A. FINANCE SOP

1. CASH RECEIPT

1. The Finance department receives daily income and daily expenditure reports from the Cashier, Bar, and Kitchen, which are then recorded weekly through spreadsheet documents.
2. Finance consolidates the cash handover summaries from the Cashier and retains them. Every week, these summaries are deposited into the company's account and transferred to the Creative Director.
3. Subsequently, Finance records the transactions in the spreadsheet report (journal).

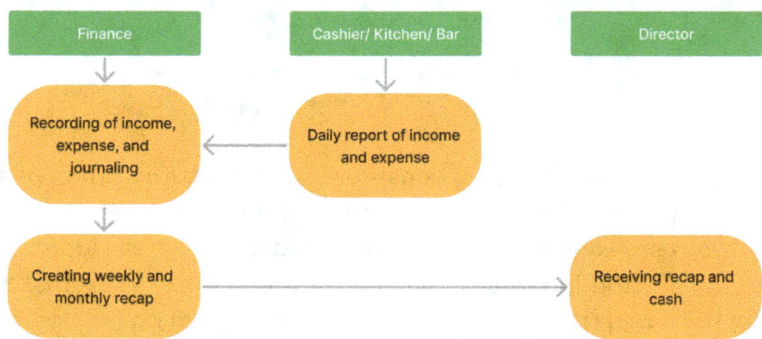

Figure 6. Finance - Cash receipt flow.

2. ORDER/ PURCHASE

1. The company or production staff determine the material needs.
2. Production staff or Finance make requests or purchases from suppliers or stores.
3. Items from the store or supplier are checked by Finance, supervisors, or verified directly by management or through documentation such as WhatsApp.
4. Finance records trade debts according to the due dates on the calendar.

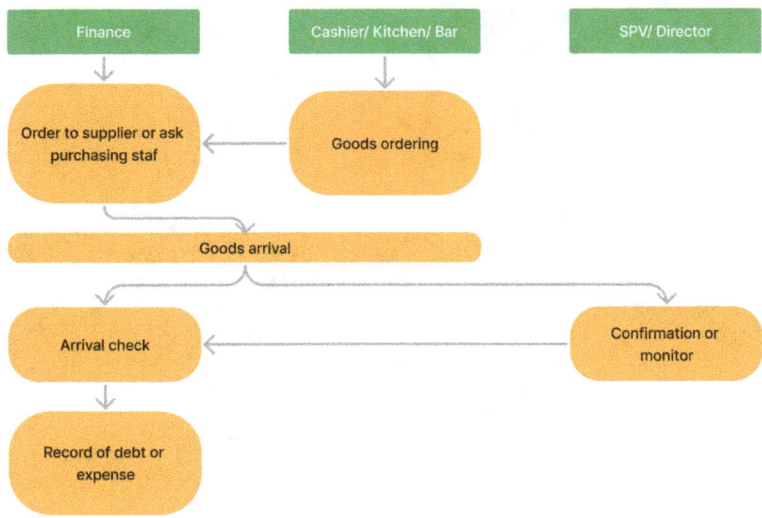

Figure 7. Finance - Order or purchase flow.

3. PAYMENT

1. Finance obtains invoices or receipts for payment purposes.
2. Finance settles invoices according to the amounts stated on the invoices/receipts, preferably on the same day. If there are specific invoices on certain dates, they may be paid according to the due date schedule.
3. If the funds for payment are insufficient, promptly withdraw from the company's account. If still insufficient, immediately contact the management.
4. Subsequently, Finance records the transactions in the spreadsheet report.

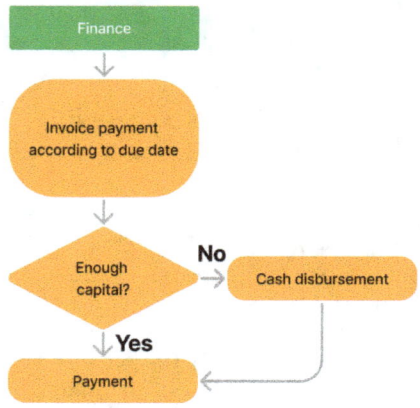

Figure 8. Finance - Payment flow.

4. REPORT

1. Finance creates and generates daily reports (revenue and customers) which are then communicated via WhatsApp to the management.
2. Every week, at the beginning of the week, Finance prepares a weekly report (revenue, customers, and expenses), reports it via WhatsApp (PDF), prints it, and places it in a folder.
3. Once a month, at the beginning of the month, Finance prepares a monthly report (revenue, customers, expenses), prints it, and places it in a folder. Especially for payroll purposes, seven days before payroll, Finance creates a prediction report (revenue, customers, expenses, salary simulation). The monthly report is distributed to all Directors (hybrid).

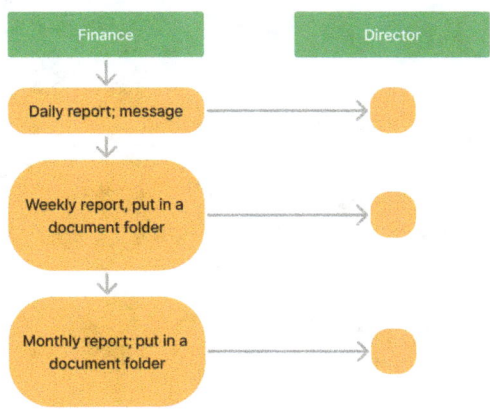

Finance - Report

Figure 9. Finance - Report flow.

5. PAYROLL

1. Finance creates a payroll simulation maximum 7 days before the payday (1st of each month; if it falls on a holiday, it can be adjusted) and reports it to the management.
2. Finance prepares the salary report based on: base salary (contract letter), deductions, incentive bonuses, and employee debts. Then, forwards the payroll documents and slips to the management.
3. Upon management acceptance, Finance promptly arranges the payroll amounts. If the cash on hand is insufficient, immediately contact management for the disbursement process.
4. On payday, Finance prints the salary slips, attendance records for salary collection, and prepares envelopes.
5. Finance digitally stores the signed attendance documents (scan).

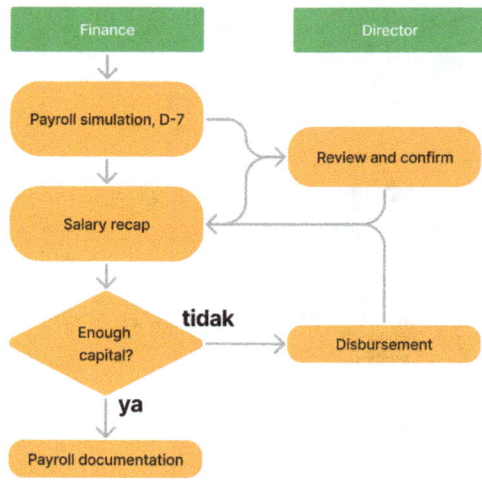

Figure 10. Finance - Payroll flow.

6. DOCUMENTS

These are the essential reports meticulously crafted and routinely utilized within the operational framework of Dhadhu Café:

1. **Daily Income Brief Report**: A brief daily's earnings, providing insights into revenue streams and performance metrics.
2. **Daily Expenditure Brief Report**: A brief daily's expenses, including procurement, operational costs, and miscellaneous expenditures, ensuring financial tracking.
3. **Daily, Weekly, and Monthly Revenue & Customer Report**: A versatile report offering a multifaceted view of revenue trends and customer engagement metrics over varying timeframes, facilitating strategic decision-making.
4. **Daily, Weekly, and Monthly Expense Report**: A detailed analysis of expenses incurred on a daily, weekly, and monthly basis, enabling effective cost management and budgetary control.
5. **Monthly Salary Simulation Report**: A predictive analysis tool forecasting monthly payroll expenses based on salary structures, deductions, and bonuses, aiding in financial planning and resource allocation.
6. **Monthly Summary Report in Slide Format**: A concise yet comprehensive presentation encapsulating key performance indicators, financial highlights, and operational insights for monthly review and strategic planning purposes.

7. **Accounts Receivable and Payable Report**: An organized record of outstanding payments receivable from customers and liabilities payable to vendors, ensuring efficient cash flow management and timely settlements.
8. **General Ledger Journal**: A meticulous record of all financial transactions, systematically categorized and documented in compliance with accounting standards, serving as the backbone of financial reporting and auditing processes.

Notes: For further guidance and detailed document templates, please refer to the dedicated section provided within our documentation resources.

B. GAME MASTER (GM) SOP

1. PREPARE

1. Arrive at the workplace 1 hour before the operational hours and check in.
2. Perform tasks according to the preparation checklist.
3. Adhere to all company regulations.
4. Arrange game components and board game shelves according to their categories.
5. Prepare game borrowing and rental forms.
6. Once the preparation is complete, send proof of the preparation checklist to the WhatsApp group.
7. The GM staff must bring and read the game summary notes.

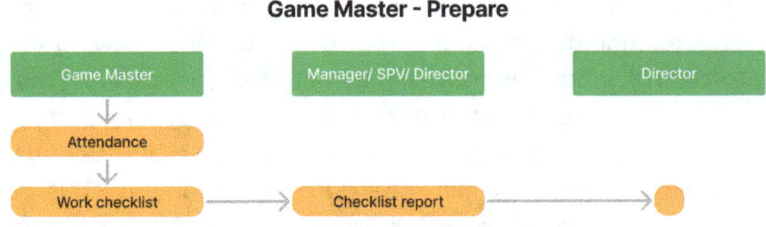

Figure 11. GM – Prepare flow.

2. CLOSING

1. Frontline staff must inform customers 30 minutes before close order (CO) for their final orders.

2. Staff are required to check, tidy up, and clean according to their respective divisions.
3. Create daily rental and borrowing reports.

Game Master - Closing

Figure 12. Game Master – Closing.

3. GAME MASTERING (GM-ing)

1. GM periodically observes if customers require assistance.
2. Customers can play one game at a time and may exchange rental games as much as they want by paying a daily game rental fee of Rp. 10,000.
3. After payment, the GM guides persuasively in selecting a game. The GM assists in directing game selection according to the customer's abilities (casual, medium, heavy).
4. After choosing a game, the GM directs the customer to fill out their details in the game rental form.
5. The GM briefly explains the flow of the game and provides understanding to the customer to tidy up after playing or before switching games. Narratives to be noted when explaining the game:
    a. Briefly explain the story, gameplay, and game components.
    b. Initiate good communication that can motivate and interest customers to play the game, for example: "This game is exciting...", "Wow, this game is cool...", "The gameplay is easy...", "It only looks difficult...".
    c. Tips: Explain simply at each player's turn, what actions they can take.
6. The GM asks the player to try playing on their own and encourages them to ask if there is anything they still don't understand.

7. The GM may play games with customers as long as the café conditions are conducive.
8. If there is damage to components, the GM must record the game title and borrower's name then report it to the management. If the fault lies with the customer, we should minimize paying fines as much as possible.

Game Master - Game Mastering

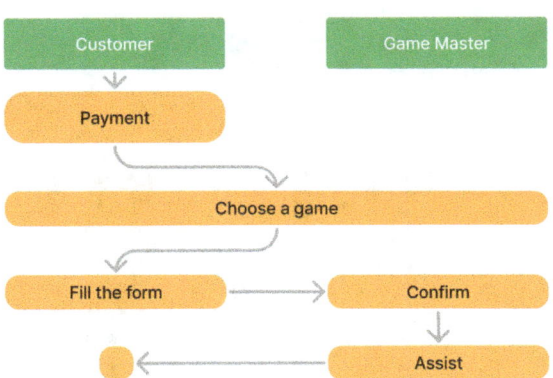

Figure 13. Game Master - Game Mastering flow.

4. CASHIER/ WAITRESS ASSISTING

1. If needed, the GM must assist the cashier and waitress as specified in the cashier/waitress SOP.
2. Tidy up tables & chairs before and after customers occupy the table.

5. MAINTENANCE

1. Every game, before or after being played, must be checked at the GM counter to assess its condition.
2. If a game is deemed unfit for play, immediately record it in the GM's logbook kept in the GM counter drawer. The information to be written includes the game title, number of players, theme, date, and damage.
3. Once a week, during non-customer hours, the assigned GM must conduct checks. Checklists and schedules will be provided by the Creative Director. Then refer back to points II and III.

4. Once a month, the GM coordinator must send an email containing a report on games deemed unfit for use.
5. The list of unfit games will be discussed during the weekly and monthly briefings.

Game Master - Maintenance

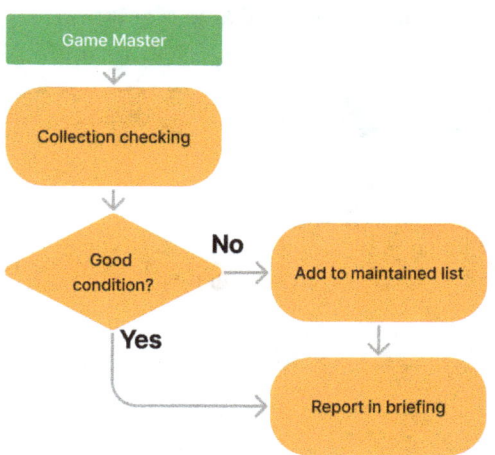

Figure 14. Game Master – Maintenance flow.

GM SOP flow – Maintenance

6. SALES & PURCHASE

1. If a customer is browsing the game collection, the GM must persuasively offer games for sale.
2. If a customer purchases a game, direct them to the cashier and record the sale.
3. Game purchases are made according to the following guidelines:
   a. Budget approximately Rp. 500,000 - Rp. 1,500,000 depending on the café's condition (taken from a portion of the game rental income of Rp. 10,000).
   b. Before requesting the purchase of a game, refer to the game master's documents or notes, including the game collection, wishlist, and damaged games. Purchases should align with these records.
   c. Priority is given to casual and medium-level games.
   d. Orders are placed via email to Nirwana Games or Hobby on a monthly basis.

4. Games that are less popular but still in good condition may be considered for sale within the price range of Retail Price/2 to Supplier Price.
5. For new game collections, before they are displayed, at least one GM must understand the gameplay, and a summary of the gameplay must be prepared. All new games must be sleeved before display.

Game Master - Sales

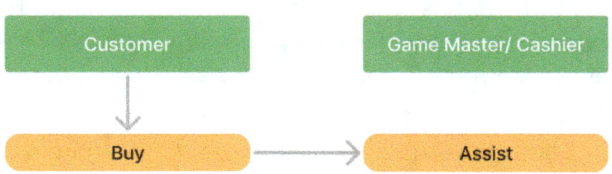

Figure 15. Game Master - Sales flow.

Game Master - Purchase

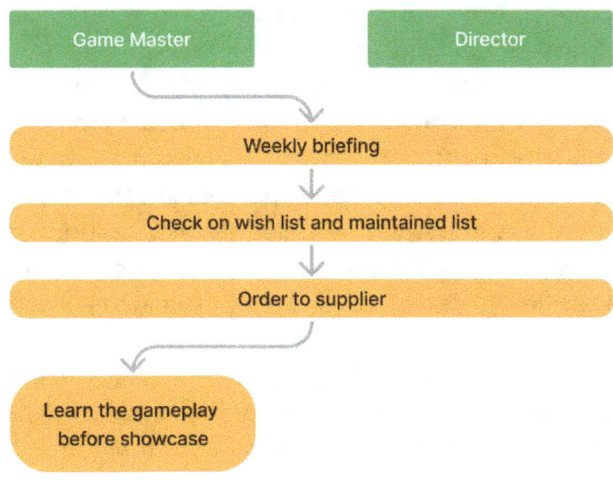

Figure 16. Game Master - Purchase flow.

7. COMPETENCY

Game masters in game Cafés need to upgrade their competencies for several reasons:

1. **Enhanced Customer Experience**: By upgrading their competencies, game masters can provide better assistance to customers. They can offer clearer explanations of game rules, suggest suitable games based on the players' preferences, and ensure smooth gameplay experiences. This leads to higher customer satisfaction and increased repeat visits.

2. **Expanded Game Library Management**: With improved competencies, game masters can effectively manage and curate the game library. They can stay updated on new game releases, understand various game mechanics, and organize the game collection more efficiently. This enables them to offer a diverse range of games that cater to different preferences and skill levels.

3. **Effective Event Management**: Game Cafés often host events such as tournaments, themed game nights, or gaming workshops. Competency upgrades allow game masters to plan and execute these events more effectively. They can develop creative event ideas, coordinate logistics, and ensure that participants have an enjoyable and memorable experience.

4. **Better Conflict Resolution**: In the gaming environment, conflicts or disputes among players may arise. Game masters with upgraded competencies are equipped to handle these situations calmly and effectively. They can mediate disputes, enforce game rules impartially, and maintain a positive gaming atmosphere.

5. **Professional Development**: Continuous learning and skill development contribute to the professional growth of game masters. By upgrading their competencies, they not only enhance their expertise in gaming but also develop valuable skills such as communication, problem-solving, and leadership. This opens up opportunities for career advancement within the gaming industry.

Overall, upgrading competencies empowers game masters to deliver exceptional customer service, manage game-related activities efficiently, and contribute positively to the overall success of the game Café. Here are the tasks we ask our GM staff to do to upgrade his competencies:

1. GM must study a minimum of 2 café collection games every week.
2. Proposing one event per month, such as playday, playtest, tournament.
3. Whenever there is a new game collection, it is mandatory to study and create a summary of the gameplay in the GM's notes.

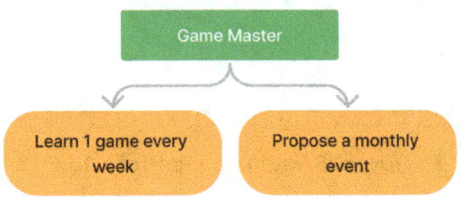

Figure 17. Game Master - Competency upgrade flow.

8. POCKET RULES FOR PLAYERS

Pocket rules, also known as reference cards or player aids, are concise summaries of the rules of a board game that players can keep handy during gameplay. These cards typically include essential information such as turn order, key actions players can take, scoring details, and any special abilities or conditions. They serve as quick references to help players remember the rules without having to consult the rulebook constantly.

1. Open the box carefully.
2. Hold the cards without folding them.
3. Check the components before and after the game.
4. Always read the rulebook!
5. Keep the components and box away from drinks, especially cold ones.
6. Return the components to their places after playing.
7. Play positively with fellow players, no bullying.
8. Wipe off any wet body parts or areas.
9. Return the game to the GM at the GM counter.

C. KITCHEN SOP

1. PREPARE

1. Arrive at the workplace 1 hour before operational hours and check-in.
2. Perform tasks according to the preparation checklist.
3. After completing the preparation, send proof of the preparation checklist to the WA group.

Kitchen - Prepare

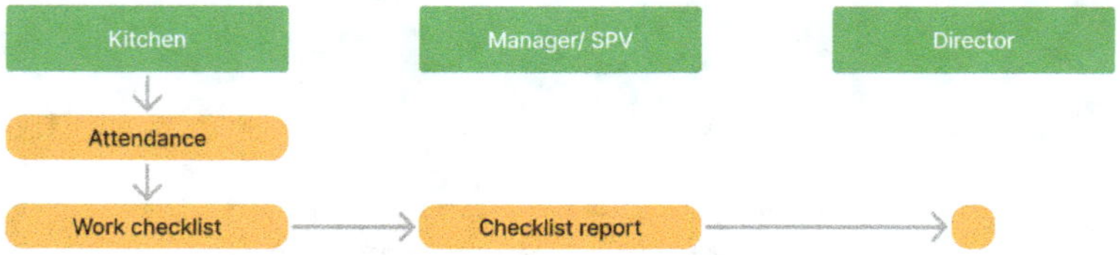

Figure 18. Kitchen - Prepare flow.

2. CLOSING

1. Perform tasks according to the closing checklist.
2. Check the raw materials for operations and record dwindling stock. Write down orders for necessary kitchen supplies for the next day, which will then be ordered from suppliers by the head kitchen or management.
3. Ensure that the stove, gas regulator, and electronic equipment are turned off.

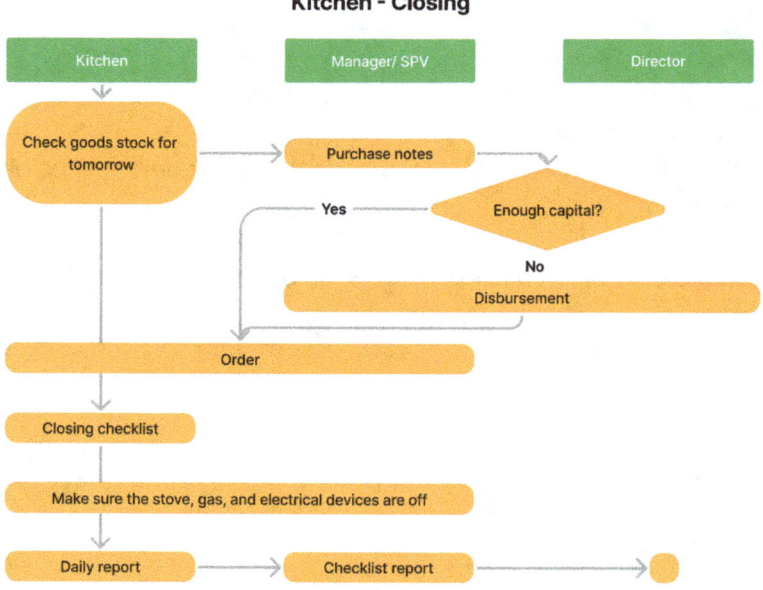

Figure 19. Kitchen - Closing flow.

3. GOODS ARRIVAL CHECK

1. Receive and inspect materials from suppliers that have been ordered, ensuring they are checked first according to the order.
2. Prepare and process raw materials.

Kitchen - Goods Arrival Check

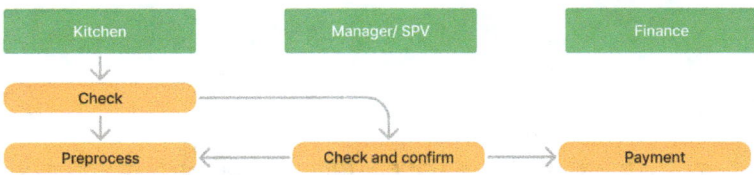

Figure 20. Kitchen - Goods arrival check.

4. PRODUCTION (COOKING)

1. Utilize the First-In-First-Out (FIFO) concept; older items should be used before newer ones to prevent accumulation or expiration (waste).
2. Follow the recipe and process standards when preparing menu items.
3. Taste-test each dish to ensure it meets the established standards before serving.
4. Clean as you go: Once finished using, immediately clean and return items to their place.

Kitchen - Production (Cook)

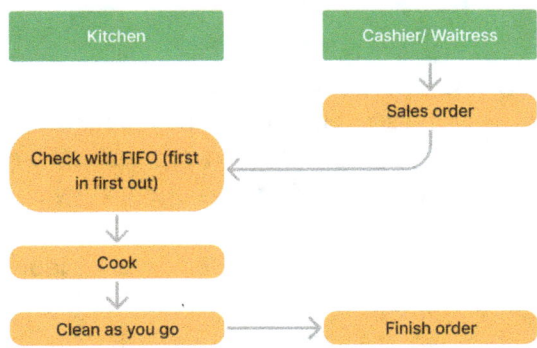

Figure 21. Kitchen - Production (Cook).

5. CLEANLINESS

1. Periodically check cooking or dining utensils in the sink. Avoid letting them pile up too much; clean them gradually.
2. Return the utensils to their respective places after washing.

D. BAR SOP

1. PREPARE

1. Arrive at the workplace 1 hour before the operational hours and clock in.
2. Perform tasks according to the preparation checklist.
3. After the preparation is complete, send proof of the preparation checklist to the WA group.

Figure 22. Bar - Prepare flow.

2. CLOSING

1. Perform tasks according to the closing checklist.
2. Check raw materials for operations and record dwindling stock. Write down orders for necessary kitchen supplies for the next day's needs, which will then be ordered from the supplier by oneself, finance, or management.
3. Ensure electronic equipment is turned off and clean.

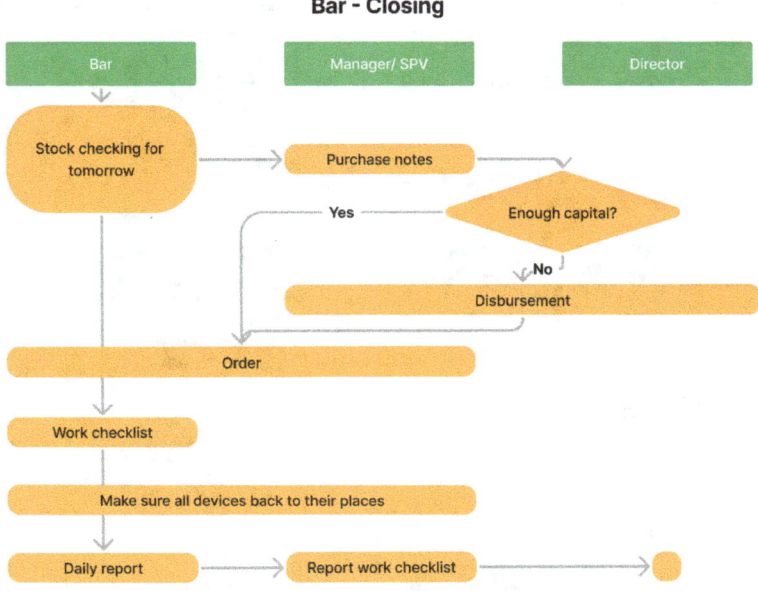

Figure 23. Bar - Closing flow.

3. GOODS ARRIVAL CHECK

1. Receive and inspect materials from suppliers that have been ordered, they should be checked first according to the order.
2. Prepare and process raw materials.

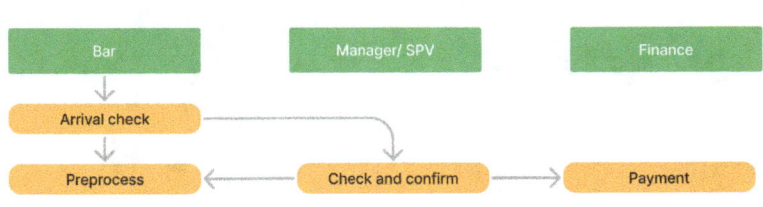

Figure 24. Bar - Goods arrival check flow.

4. PRODUCTION

1. Use the First-In-First-Out (FIFO) concept, where older items should be used before newer ones. Avoid accumulation or expiration (waste).
2. Follow the recipe and process standards that have been established when making menu items.

3. Taste-test every dish made to ensure that the flavor meets the standard before serving.
4. Clean as you go = once finished using, clean immediately and return to its place.

Bar - Production

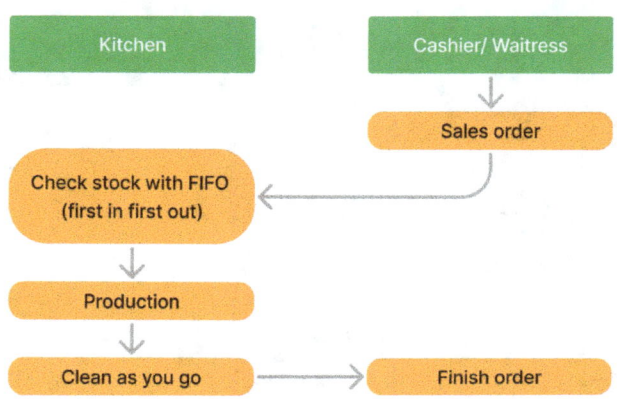

Figure 25. Bar - Production flow.

5. CLEANLINESS

1. Periodically check the cooking or eating utensils in the sink. Do not let them pile up too much, work on them gradually.
2. After washing the utensils, return them to their respective places.

E. CASHIER SOP

1. PREPARE

1. Come to work 1 hour before the operational hours and mark attendance.
2. Perform tasks according to the preparation checklist.
3. Obey all company regulations.
4. Tidy up the counter and prepare cashier equipment.
5. After preparation is completed, send evidence of the preparation checklist to the WA group.
6. Staff must read the stock and sold-out notes.

Cashier - Prepare

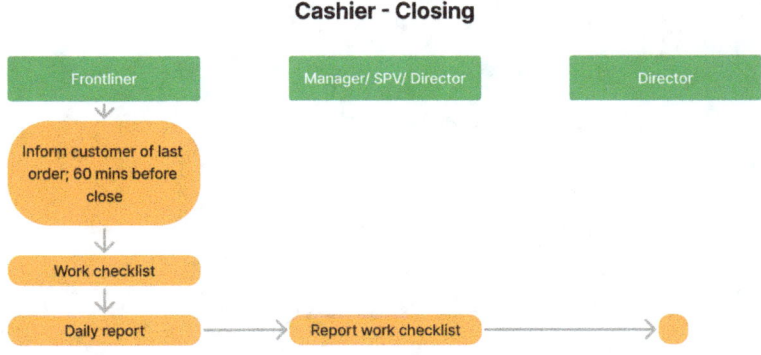

Figure 26. Cashier - Prepare flow.

2. CLOSING

1. Frontline staff must inform customers 30 minutes before the close order (CO) for the last order.
2. Staff must check, tidy up, and clean according to their respective divisions.
3. Create daily income reports. Any discrepancies are entirely the responsibility of the cashier.

Cashier - Closing

Figure 27. Cashier - Closing flow.

3. SALES

1. Say greetings as stated in the Company's Hospitality Rules:
    a. Always greet customers when they enter the café, such as "Welcome to Dhadhu, kak (guys)!"
    b. Try to ask for permission before communicating with customers and express gratitude.

    c.   Receive and hand over any items to customers using both hands if possible.

2.   Customer ordering:
    a.   Allow customers to choose from the hanging menu or the menu on the table.
    b.   Take note of customer orders and recommend menu items.
    c.   Repeat customer orders and complete payment.
    d.   Allow customers to sit and inquire about table positions.
    e.   The cashier provides the order structure to the bar and kitchen.

3.   Customers can order modified menu items according to their preferences due to allergies, etc.

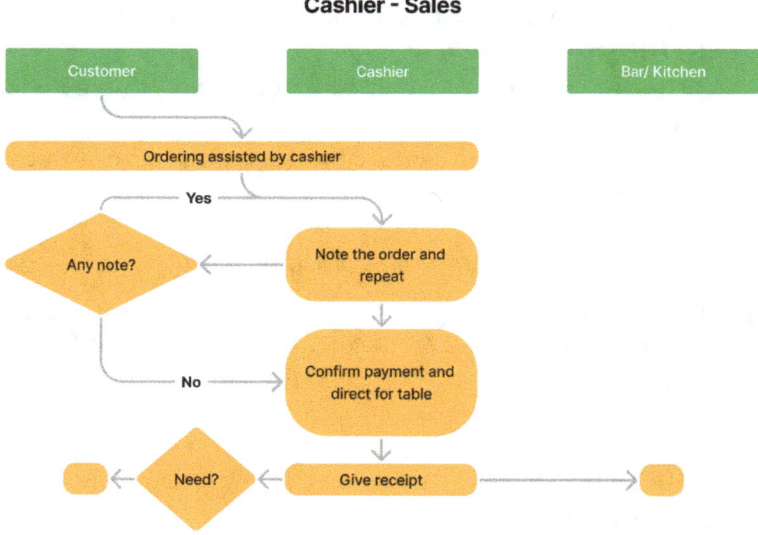

Figure 28. Cashier - Sales flow.

4. EXPENSE

1.   All needs or expenses using the cashier's money must be recorded in the cashier's logbook and daily income report at closing.

2.   For purchases, minimize the use of cashier's money as much as possible. Use the capital provided to the kitchen division, Rp. 1,000,000. If the kitchen's capital runs out, then cashier's money can be used.

Cashier - Expense

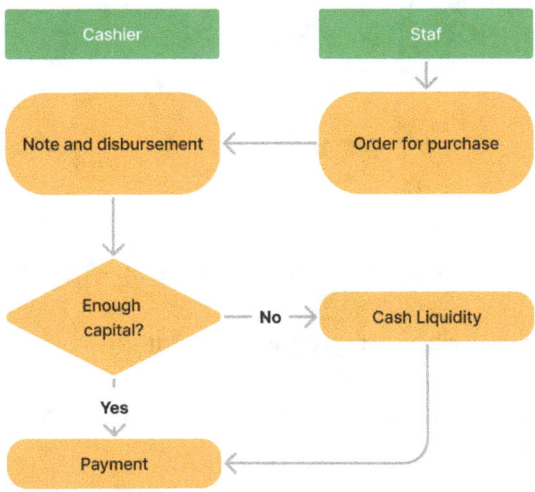

Figure 29. Cashier - Expense flow.

5. ASSISTING WAITRESS, RUNNER, & BARISTA

1. Arrange the tables and chairs before and after the customers occupy them.
2. Periodically, staff check the customers' tables to look for empty or used eating utensils.
3. If there are eating utensils that can be taken or cleaned, it is advisable to say a phrase like "Excuse me, may I take the used utensils? Thank you."
4. If necessary, the cashier assists in making drinks at the bar or snacks in the kitchen.

6. COMPETENCY

1. Cashiers must know and be able to use all cashier equipment such as the POS (Point of Sales) Majoo application, money drawer, EDC, QRIS.
2. Every week, cashiers must play and learn at least 1 new game, especially casual games like Chicky Boom, Santorini, Baobab, etc.
3. Every cashier must be able to make simple drinks such as:
   a. Non-Coffee: Tea, Flavored Tea, Chocolate, Hazelnut Chocolate, Mojito.

b. Coffee: Black Coffee, Ginger Coffee, Coffee with Milk, Americano.

F. MARKETING SOP

1. PREPARE

1. Arrive at the workplace 1 hour before the operational hours and clock in.
2. Perform tasks according to the preparation checklist.
3. Adhere to all company rules.
4. After preparation is complete, send proof of preparation checklist to the WA group.

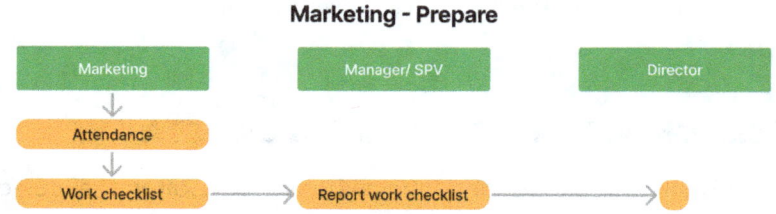

Figure 30. Marketing - Prepare flow.

2. EDITORIAL PLAN

1. Designing content and event planning with an activity calendar, including a Google calendar.
2. Every month, the marketing team submits an event proposal at least once to the management.
3. Every month, submit proposals for influencers or figures for marketing purposes.

Marketing - Editorial Plan

Figure 31. Marketing - Editorial plan flow.

3. RELATIONSHIP MANAGEMENT

1. Managing contacts, inquiries, and maintaining good relationships with customers and the community.
2. Sending invitations when the café will hold an event through social media and email.
3. Handling advertising.
4. Serving as a representative for meetings with partners.
5. Conducting door-to-door marketing for B2B partners at least once a month.
6. Do a community research.

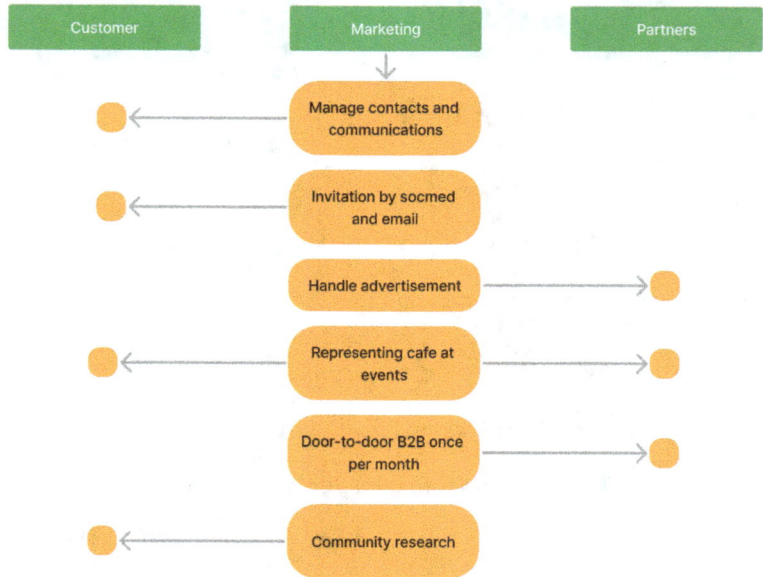

Figure 32. Marketing – Relationship management flow.

4. MARKETING RESEARCH

1. Every month, marketing must visit at least 2 Cafés with the potential for comparative analysis.
2. Analyzing social media development every week and every month.
3. Analyzing potential communities to become partners or customers.

Figure 33. Marketing – Research flow.

G. SUPERVISOR (SPV) SOP

1. PREPARE

1. Arrive at the workplace 1 hour before operational hours and clock in.
2. Perform tasks according to the preparation checklist.
3. Adhere to all company regulations.
4. Ensure all divisions complete the preparation checklist.
5. Read the management book for 10 minutes.

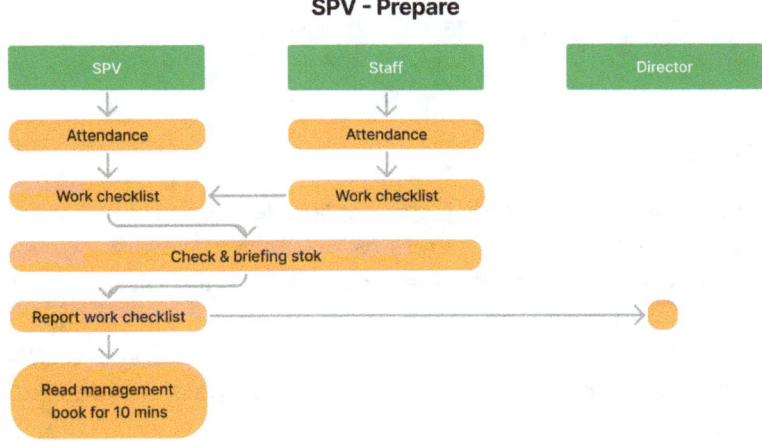

Figure 34. SPV - Prepare flow.

2. CLOSING

1. Frontliner staff must inform customers 30 minutes before the close order (CO) for the last order.
2. Staff must check, tidy up, and clean according to their respective divisions.
3. Receive and check the daily income report. Then, relay it to the management through WhatsApp.

SPV - Closing

Frontliner	Manager/ SPV/ Director	Director

Inform customer of last order; 60 mins before close

Work checklist → Work checklist

Daily report → Report work checklist →

Figure 35. SPV - Closing flow.

3. SUPERVISION

1. Responsible for enforcing the applicable rules and regulations and overseeing the café's operations.
2. Familiarize oneself with the workflow of each division and assist divisions in need.
3. Provide operational checklist reports for preparation and closing.
4. Resolve work conflicts personally. If not possible, address them internally within the division.
5. Offer advice and motivation to staff.
6. Ensure cleanliness in all café areas (indoor, production, restrooms, prayer room, outdoor).
7. Report a summary of daily operations via WhatsApp.
8. Responsible for the staff regeneration process.

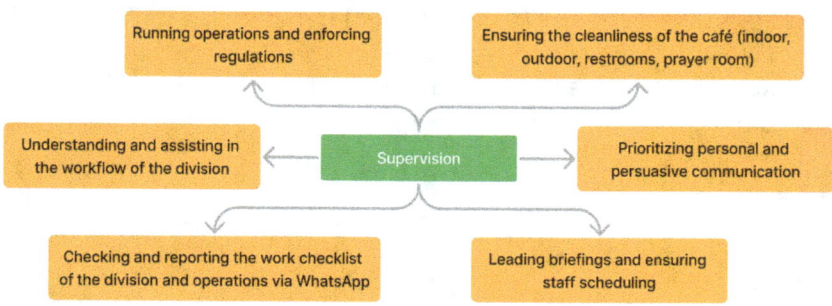

Supervision Responsibility

Figure 36. SPV - Supervision responsibilities.

4. BRIEFING & REPORT

1. Serve as the minute-taker or leader during briefings.
2. Report daily, weekly, and monthly reports.
3. Share insights from management books read for 10 minutes every week.

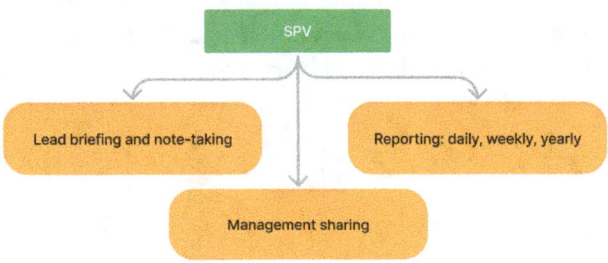

Figure 37. SPV - Briefing & reporting flow.

V. WORKING CHECKLIST

Checklists or protocols are frequently used to prevent human errors in demanding work settings (Borchard et al., 2012; Degani & Wiener, 1991). When utilized, they often bring about significant changes both in the systems and the culture of operating teams. These changes foster better communication and teamwork by spreading responsibility across the entire team, rather than relying solely on hierarchy, which ultimately boosts job satisfaction. Moreover, checklists help clarify each team member's role.

A. FRONTLINER (CASHIER, GM, BAR) CHECKLIST

Table 1. Frontliner working checklist.

Frontliner Checklist (Cashier, GM dan Barista)								
Prepare		Mon	Tue	Wed	Thu	Fri	Sat	Sun
1	**Login Attendance**							
2	Cleaning and tidying up the counter							
3	Cleaning and tidying up tables & chairs							
4	Cleaning board game shelves							
5	Wiping front door glass							
6	Emptying and refilling trash bags							
7	Refilling tissue & hand sanitizer							
8	Setting up white tables, ashtrays, outdoor tissue							
9	Sweeping & mopping indoor floors							
10	Sweeping & mopping outdoor floors							
11	Wiping dining utensils							
12	Turning on EDC & Sound system							
13	Menu stock briefing							
14	Spraying insect repellent & room freshener							
15	Opening curtains & adjusting signboard							
Closing		Mon	Tue	Wed	Thu	Fri	Sat	Sun

1	Providing close order information to customers								
2	Closing curtains and signboards								
3	Cleaning and tidying up tables and chairs								
4	Taking out trash								
5	Cleaning and tidying up the counter								
6	Ensuring dining utensils are cleaned up								
7	Placing white tables, ashtrays, and tissue								
8	Checking & refilling thermal paper								
9	Daily report								
10	Washing trays								
11	**Logging out attendance**								
12	Turning off and tidying up EDC, tablet, PC, and sound system								

B. BAR CHECKLIST

Table 2. Bar working checklist.

Bar Checklist								
Prepare		Mon	Tue	Wed	Thu	Fri	Sat	Sun
1	**Login attendance**							
2	Preparing glasses and bar tables							
3	Calibration							
4	Cleaning the bar floor							
5	Preparing stock materials							
6	Cleaning the chiller							
7	Preparing a cloth							
8	Cleaning the middle rack							
9	Wiping the side door glass							
10	Menu stock briefing							
11	Cleaning and tidying up tables & chairs							
12	Sweeping & mopping indoor floor							
Closing		Mon	Tue	Wed	Thu	Fri	Sat	Sun
1	Washing all utensils and glasses							
2	Cleaning the coffee machine							

3	Cleaning the bar table									
4	Washing cloths									
5	Cleaning the sink									
6	Taking out the trash									
7	Checking stock materials									
8	Sweeping and mopping the bar floor									
9	**Logout attendance**									

C. KITCHEN CHECKLIST

Table 3. Kitchen working checklist.

Kitchen Checklist								
Prepare		Mon	Tue	Wed	Thu	Fri	Sat	Sun
1	**Login attendance**							
2	Preparing stock materials							
3	Menu stock briefing							
4	Cooking rice							
5	Tidying up utensils & sink							
6	Ensuring and refilling snack flags							
Closing		Mon	Tue	Wed	Thu	Fri	Sat	Sun
1	Washing dishes and kitchen utensils							
2	Cleaning the sink							
3	Taking out the trash							
4	Wiping ceramic walls							
5	Cleaning the blower							
6	Cleaning and tidying up plate racks							
7	Cleaning spice containers							
8	Cleaning the chiller							
9	Cleaning the freezer							
10	Sweeping and mopping the floor							
11	Checking stock materials							
12	**Logout attendance**							

D. MARKETING CHECKLIST

Table 4. Marketing working checklist.

Marketing Checklist		Mon	Tue	Wed	Thu	Fri	Sat	Sun
1	**Login attendance**							
2	Cleaning the work environment							
3	Sending quotation proposals to B2B partners							
4	Sending marketing emails to customers							
5	Analyzing market trends via Google and social media and creating reports							
6	Creating an editorial plan							
7	Creating marketing content							

E. FINANCE CHECKLIST

Table 5. Finance working checklist.

Finance Checklist		Mon	Tue	Wed	Thu	Fri	Sat	Sun
1	**Login attendance**							
2	Cleaning the work environment							
3	Paying bills							
4	Recording transactions in the journal							
5	Creating weekly or monthly financial reports							

F. SPV CHECKLIST

Table 6. SPV daily working checklist.

SPV Checklist									
No	Activities	Mon	Tue	Wed	Thu	Fri	Sat	Sun
1	Checklists for preparing cashier, bar, kitchen, and duty roster							
2	Menu stock check, FIFO							

3	Utensil equipment check (spoons, plastic, cups, stickers)								
4	Daily Report								
5	Closing checklist check								

Table 7. SPV weekly working checklist.

SPV Weekly Checklist						
No	Activities	Week 1	Week 2	Week 3	Week 4	Week 5
1	Weekly Report (marketing, game master)					
2	Laundry (apron, prayer clothes, prayer rug)					
3	Check Perfume, Baygon, First Aid Kit, Soap, Vixal, Tissue, Camphor					
4	Staff experiment materials (Rp. 50,000)					
5	Briefing and minutes					

Table 8. SPV monthly working checklist.

SPV Monthly Checklist													
No	Activities	Jan	Feb	Mar	Apr	May	Jun	Jul	Aug	Sep	Oct	Nov	Dec
1	General Cleaning												
2	Monthly meeting and briefing												

G. CLEANLINESS DUTY SCHEDULE

Table 9. Cleanliness duty schedule.

Duty Schedule								
Prepare		Mon	Tue	Wed	Thu	Fri	Sat	Sun
1	Cleaning toilet and prayer room							
2	Warming up the genset (5 min)							
3	Whipping the window							

VI. EMPLOYMENT CONTRACT

An employment contract, also known as a contract of employment, is a legal agreement used in labor law to define the rights and duties of both parties involved. It typically involves an agreement between an employee and an employer. The contract is based on the idea of authority, where the employee agrees to follow the employer's directives, and in return, the employer agrees to provide compensation, usually in the form of a specified wage (Simon, 1951). It's important for a contract to benefit both parties. As an employer, your contract should motivate your employees to enhance their performance and grow within the company. Below is an example or template of an employment contract letter.

Table 10. Employment contract letter.

EMPLOYMENT AGREEMENT
NUMBER: <DIRECTORATE/SUBJECT/MONTH/YEAR/NUMBER>

The undersigned:

Name   : _ _ _ _ _ _ _ _ _ _
Position   : _ _ _ _ _ _ _ _ _ _
Address   : _ _ _ _ _ _ _ _ _ _

Hereby acting on behalf of the management of Dhadhu Board Game Café (PT. Nagara Kaya Karsa) domiciled at Jl. Timoho Raya No. 25-26 Bulusan, Tembalang, Semarang, hereinafter referred to as the **FIRST PARTY**.

Name   : _ _ _ _ _ _ _ _ _ _
Place/Date of Birth : _ _ _ _ _ _ _ _ _ _
Last Education   : _ _ _ _ _ _ _ _ _ _
Gender   : _ _ _ _ _ _ _ _ _ _
Religion   : _ _ _ _ _ _ _ _ _ _
Address   : _ _ _ _ _ _ _ _ _ _
ID Card Number   : _ _ _ _ _ _ _ _ _ _
Phone Number   : _ _ _ _ _ _ _ _ _ _

In this matter, acting for and on behalf of oneself, hereinafter referred to as the **SECOND PARTY**.

On this day of _ _ _ _ _ _ _ _ _ _ _ _ _ _, _ _ _ _ _ _ _ _ _ _ _ _ _, the undersigned parties have agreed to be bound by the terms and conditions of the employment agreement as follows:

ARTICLE ONE
The FIRST PARTY declares to accept the SECOND PARTY as an employee at the company Dhadhu Board Game Café located at Jl. Timoho Raya No. 25-26 Bulusan, Tembalang, Semarang, and the SECOND PARTY hereby declares their willingness.

ARTICLE TWO

The SECOND PARTY will be placed as (fulltime/part-time) _____ in the division
_____. If deemed necessary and desired, the FIRST PARTY may assign
the SECOND PARTY to perform other tasks and duties considered more suitable and appropriate by the
FIRST PARTY, provided that they remain within the Dhadhu Board Game Café company premises.

ARTICLE THREE

1. The contract period for full-time employees is set for _____,
   calculated from the date of entry of the SECOND PARTY into employment.
2. The contract period for part-time employees is set for _____,
   calculated from the date of entry of the SECOND PARTY into employment.

ARTICLE FOUR

1. Specifically for Full-time employees, the FIRST PARTY must provide a salary to the SECOND PARTY
   every month, to be paid on the agreed date each month after deducting income tax in
   accordance with Indonesian tax regulations, assuming a working day of 26 days each month.
   The salary details are as follows:
   a. Basic Salary   : _____
   b. Allowance   : _____
   c. Bonus   : _____ (If daily targets are met)
   d. Meal Allowance   : _____
2. Specifically for Part-time employees, the FIRST PARTY must provide a salary to the SECOND PARTY
   calculated based on the number of working hours multiplied by the agreed nominal amount of
   (Rp. _____) [_____], to be paid by
   the FIRST PARTY on the agreed date each month after deducting income tax in accordance with
   Indonesian tax regulations.
3. Salary details are attached in the addendum.

ARTICLE FIVE

In accordance with applicable labor regulations, the effective working hours are [9 nine] hours per
week with a total of 7 [Seven] working days per week, as detailed follow: Monday to Sunday, the working
hours are from 14.00 [fourteen] to 23.00 [twenty-three] with a rest period of [30 minutes], subject to
agreement. Each staff will work for 6 [six] working days per week.

ARTICLE SIX

1. The FIRST PARTY must provide meal allowances to the SECOND PARTY once a day for each day
   the SECOND PARTY works. Meals can be provided in the form of food or allowances.
2. The SECOND PARTY is entitled to an additional meal if working overtime, either in the form of food
   or allowances.

ARTICLE SEVEN

1. Whenever possible, work activities shall be conducted only during working hours. If there is work
   that needs to be completed immediately or is urgent, and the SECOND PARTY is required to work
   overtime, the FIRST PARTY will pay the SECOND PARTY for the overtime work according to the
   calculation of working hours (from the basic salary) for each overtime hour.
2. Overtime wages will be combined with the salary payment received by the FIRST PARTY on the
   last day of each month.

ARTICLE EIGHT

1. Each employee is entitled to leave as stated in the company's rule book.
2. Leave requests on working days must be submitted by each employee no later than 7 [seven]
   days before the scheduled leave, with approval in the form of a signature and permission from
   the relevant immediate superior.

ARTICLE NINE

The FIRST PARTY is obliged to bear the cost of medical treatment and care if the SECOND PARTY falls ill
or requires medical treatment in accordance with the terms, regulations, and provisions established
by the company.

ARTICLE TEN

1. The SECOND PARTY expresses readiness to comply with and adhere to all the rules and regulations of Dhadhu Board Game Café established by the FIRST PARTY.
2. Violations of the above-mentioned regulations may result in the following actions against the SECOND PARTY:
   a. Suspension, or
   b. Written Warning (WW)
   c. Termination of Employment (TE), or
   d. Other forms of punishment with reference to the Governing Regulations.

ARTICLE ELEVEN

During the term of this employment agreement, the SECOND PARTY is not allowed to engage in concurrent work in any other company for any reason whatsoever, unless the SECOND PARTY has obtained written consent from the FIRST PARTY.

ARTICLE TWELVE

1. The FIRST PARTY has the right at any time to terminate this employment agreement, provided that written notice is given to the SECOND PARTY without any obligation to explain the reasons. In this matter, the FIRST PARTY must provide the unpaid salary to the SECOND PARTY, the amount and arrangements of which shall refer to the applicable Government Regulations.
2. If the SECOND PARTY resigns before the end of the contract period, the SECOND PARTY is obliged to reimburse the remaining months' salary to the FIRST PARTY for the current period.
3. The FIRST PARTY has the right at any time to change the percentage (%) of the salary given to employees up to 90% (ninety percent) if the minimum monthly turnover target is not met as stated in the addendum.

ARTICLE THIRTEEN

This employment agreement will terminate automatically if the SECOND PARTY passes away or for any other reasons deemed acceptable by the FIRST PARTY.

ARTICLE FOURTEEN

This employment agreement will automatically be terminated if due to circumstances or situations that are compelling, such as natural disasters, rebellions, wars, riots, Government Regulations, or anything else that renders this employment agreement impossible to fulfill.

ARTICLE FIFTEEN

1. In the event of a dispute between the two parties, it will be resolved through mutual consultation to achieve consensus.
2. If an agreement cannot be reached through the method described in clause 1 of this article, both parties agree to settle the matter through legal procedures, by choosing the legal jurisdiction at the Semarang High Court.

ARTICLE SIXTEEN

This agreement is hereby made, agreed upon, and signed in duplicate, each having the same legal force and both originals and copies stamped adequately. One copy is held by the FIRST PARTY, and the other is for the SECOND PARTY.

Signed in : Semarang
Date : _____

FIRST PARTY   **SECOND PARTY**

DIRECTOR   -----------------------

VII. STAFF EVALUATION

A performance review, also known as an evaluation, is a regular and organized process where an employee's job performance is assessed and recorded. The evaluation is used to assess an individual employee's job performance and productivity in relation to certain pre-established criteria and organizational objectives (Manasa & Reddy, 2009). As performance evaluators, we use the following simple factors as determinants of the performance index. In more mature companies, the term Key Performance Index (KPI) is often used to evaluate the employee's work quality. It offers many methods to do the assessment. However, because of my capability to handle almost everything on the director level, we just want to keep everything as simple as possible.

A. PEER FEEDBACK

Usually, we use a questionnaire distributed during the monthly briefing to all staff to provide assessments of other staff members. Typically, we employ a Likert scale of 1-5 to determine the performance ratings of staff. Here are some example questions found on the questionnaire:

Table 11. Peer evaluation questionnaire.

Date   :
Name   :
Staff being assessed :
Average score   :

*Fill in your assessment of your colleague using the scale (1: very poor - 5 excellent).

1.   How would you rate the quality of your colleague's work?

Very Poor	Poor	Neutral	Good	Very Good

2.   How would you rate your colleague's speed in completing tasks?

Very Poor	Poor	Neutral	Good	Very Good

3.   How does your colleague communicate with you and others?

Very Poor	Poor	Neutral	Good	Very Good

4.   How do you rate your colleague's cleanliness, tidiness, personal hygiene, and work environment?

Very Poor	Poor	Neutral	Good	Very Good

5.   Feedback:

B. CUSTOMER FEEDBACK

Assuming that there are no significant complaints or feedback from customers via WhatsApp, email, or Google reviews, we evaluate the employee with a score of 4 (good). If there are positive reviews, we rate it as excellent (5). However, if there are negative reviews, we can rate it as fair (2) or very poor (1). These scores will then be averaged with peer feedback.

C. MANAGEMENT (DIRECT) OBSERVATION

Conducting direct observations is certainly challenging because we must maintain objectivity. We can use metrics such as: quality and accuracy of work. For example:
1. Staff initiative to provide input or feedback.
2. Staff contribution within and beyond their job description.

D. EVALUATION RESULT

The results from peer feedback, customer complaints, and direct observation will be averaged to obtain the average performance index for all staff. These results will then be compiled into a ranking or leaderboard. If a staff member's score is equal to or above 4, then they are considered good and may be considered for monthly incentives. If a staff member has an average index below 4, they should be called in for a personal discussion and asked about operational challenges. Additionally, as management, we must cross-check with other staff in the field to validate the accuracy.

Formula:

$$Employee\ of\ the\ month = \frac{peer\ feedback + customer\ complaints + observation}{3}$$

Incentives can be given in the form of vouchers or cash ranging from Rp. 50,000 to Rp. 100,000.

Notes: You need to consider the circumstances on your own café to construct the formula.

VIII. MENU RECIPE

A. FOODS

Due to the confidentiality of the recipes, we only provide two samples of each menu item for main courses, snacks, coffee-based drinks, and non-coffee-based drinks.

1. MAIN COURSE

Table 12. Menu recipe: Chicken pop.

Menu: Chicken Pop					
Method: fry			Plate: Bowl		
No	**Ingredients**	**Quantity**	**Unit**	**Type**	**Note**
1	Chicken thigh	1 (75-80 gr)	Portion	Core	
2	Chicken pop flour	50 (1 scoop)	Gr	Core	Full
3	Egg	½	Item	Core	As needed
4	Rice	1 (150 gr)	Bowl	Core	
5	Nori	2	Piece	Garnish	
6	Pickle	1	Tbs	Garnish	
7	Spicy sauce/ Sambal matah	1-2	Tbs	Core	Full

Steps:
1. Coat the bite-sized chicken pieces with egg batter, then coat with chicken pop flour twice, then fry until golden brown.
2. Prepare a bowl of rice and garnish.
3. Once the chicken is cooked, serve it in the bowl with rice and garnish.
4. Serve with sambal sauce or sambal matah.

Sambal Matah (approx. 5 servings):
- 200 gr Shallots
- 1 stalk Lemongrass
- 10 Red bird's eye chilies
- 5 leaves Kaffir lime leaves
- 3 tablespoons hot oil
- 1gr Shrimp paste
- Pepper as needed

Table 13. Menu recipe: Combo wings.

Menu: Combo Wings					
Method: boil, fry			Plate: Long plate		
No	**Ingredients**	**Quantity**	**Unit**	**Type**	**Note**
1	Chicken wings	1 (140 gr)	Portion	Core	
2	Basic flour	50	Gr	Core	As needed
3	Basic flour batter	25	Gr	Core	As needed

4	Rice	1 (150 gr)	Bowl	Core	
5	Tomato	2	Slice	Garnish	
6	Pickle	1	Tbs	Garnish	
7	BBQ sauce	1 (70 gr)	Scoop	Sauce	

Steps:
1. Coat the chicken wings with basic flour batter and then with the basic flour batter mixture, then fry until golden brown.
2. Prepare a plate of rice and garnish.
3. Prepare BBQ sauce, cook onions and garlic until fragrant, then add BBQ sauce, put the cooked chicken wings into the sauce.
4. Serve the wings on the prepared plate.

2. SIDE DISH

Table 14. Menu recipe: Waffle.

Menu: Waffle

Method: pan bake   Plate: plate

No	Ingredients	Quantity	Unit	Type	Note
1	Waffle	1	Portion	Core	
2	Chocolate condensed milk	10	Ml	Condiment	As needed
3	Ice cream	1	Scoop	Condiment	As needed
4	Simple syrup	10	Ml	Core	As needed
5	Strawberry	2	Slice	Topping	

Steps:
1. Heat the waffle in the microwave for 1 minute at 399°F.
2. Cut the waffle diagonally into 2 pieces, place it on a plate garnished with chocolate condensed milk.
3. Place ice cream on top of the waffle and drizzle with simple s

Table 15. Menu recipe: Dhadhu toast.

Menu: Dhadhu Toast

Method: pan fry   Plate: plate

No	Ingredients	Quantity	Unit	Type	Note
1	Bread (roti bandung)	1	Portion	Core	
2	Butter	50	Gr	Core	As needed
3	Jam	35	Gr	Core	As needed
4	Chocolate condensed milk	-	Ml	Core	As needed
5	Cheddar cheese	2	Slice	Topping	As needed
6	Chocolate sprinkles	1	Tbs	Topping	

Steps:
1. Spread butter and jam on the Bandung bread.
2. Heat the pan and add butter, wait until it melts.
3. Toast the bread until browned.
4. Prepare a plate, garnish with Chocolate Sweetened Condensed Milk.
5. Cut the cooked bread into 6 pieces, serve on the plate.
6. Garnish with grated cheese and chocolate sprinkles.

B. BEVERAGES

Due to the confidentiality of the recipes, we only provide two samples of each menu item for main courses, snacks, coffee-based drinks, and non-coffee-based drinks.

1. NON-COFFEE

Table 16. Menu recipe: Mojito virgin.

Menu: Mojito Virgin					
Method: layer			Cup: slim		
No	Ingredients	Quantity	Unit	Type	Note
1	Simple syrup	15	ml	Core	
2	Lime	1	1/2	Core	Slice
3	Mint syrup	20	ml	Core	
4	Soda plain	120	ml	Core	
5	Es batu	50	ml	Core	As needed
Steps: 1. Pour ingredients 1-4 into the cup. 2. Put ice cube into the cup. 3. Pour soda into the cup. 4. Place a lime garnish on top of it.					

Table 17. Menu recipe: Strawberry float.

Menu: Strawberry Float					
Method: blend			Gelas: slim high		
No	Ingredients	Quantity	Unit	Type	Note
1	Strawberry	3	Item	Core	
2	Simple syrup	10	ml	Core	
3	Strawberry syrup	20	ml	Core	
4	Shaved ice	150	ml	Core	
5	Strawberry ice cream	1	scoop	Core	
6	Water	100	ml	Core	
Steps: 1. Blend ingredients 1-4 for 1 minutes until mixed. 2. Pour into the cup. 3. Place a scoop of ice cream on top of it.					

2. COFFEE-BASED

Table 18. Menu recipe: Black avocado.

Menu: Black Avocado					
Method: layer			Gelas: mug		
No	Ingredients	Quantity	Unit	Type	Note
1	Simple syrup	25	ml	Core	

2	UHT milk	100	ml	Core	
3	Chocolate Ice Cream	100	ml	Core	As needed
4	Single shot espresso	1	Single	Core	
5	Ice cubes	100	ml	Core	As needed
6	Avocado	1/8	Slice	Core	
7	Chocolate sauce	10	ml	Garnish	As needed

Steps:

1. Pour simple syrup and UHT milk into the glass.
2. Add ice cubes to the glass.
3. Pour espresso into the glass.
4. Add chocolate ice cream and sliced avocado.
5. Top with chocolate sauce.

C. PLATING

Plating is important for F&B business. It enhances the quality of the menu and gives better first impression.

Table 19. Main course plating examples.

MAIN COURSE

Chicken Curry | Teka Teki Katsu

Pandora Bowl	Tori-tori

Table 20. Side dish platting examples.

SIDE DISH	
 Mushroom Tower	 Pancake
 Roti Bakar	 Waffle

Table 21. Beverage cupping examples.

BEVERAGES	
Kopi Susu Aren	Cappuccino
Strawberry Float	Mojito

IX. DOCUMENT TEMPLATES

Considerably, this is one of important parts of this book. In this chapter, I show you document templates you can use and adjust according to your own environment. You can use a spreadsheet document software like Microsoft Office, Libre Office, or Google Sheet.

A. FINANCE DOCUMENT TEMPLATES

1. REVENUE (DAILY, WEEKLY, MONTHLY, YEARLY)

Table 22. Example of monthly revenue report for August 2023.

Date	F&B Sales	Game Rent	Game Sales	Voucher	Gross	Non-cash	Cash	Actual	Customers
01 August 2023	292,000				292,000	265,000	27,000	3,000	9
02 August 2023	411,000				411,000	197,000	214,000	178,000	11
03 August 2023	406,600				406,600	299,800	106,800	82,800	15
04 August 2023	1,521,000				1,521,000	574,000	947,000	792,000	12
05 August 2023	1,931,600				1,931,600	1,041,000	890,600	633,600	43
...	...	...	...	...	...	...	...	...	...
26 August 2023	2,357,800				2,357,800	1,510,200	847,600	684,100	58
27 August 2023	1,054,500				1,054,500	803,000	251,500	144,500	39
28 August 2023	617,000				617,000	219,000	398,000	173,500	27
29 August 2023	2,650,500				2,650,500	2,006,100	644,400	576,400	94
30 August 2023	1,507,000				1,507,000	809,000	698,000	662,000	60
31 August 2023	1,663,000				1,663,000	1,331,000	332,000	259,500	111
Average	1,198,613	70,000			1,200,871	730,248	470,623	362,303	37
Total					37,227,000	22,637,700	14,589,300	11,231,400	1,155

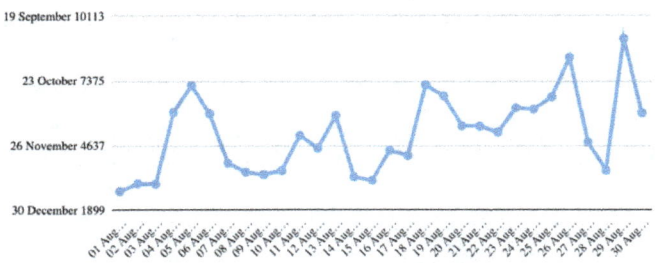

Figure 38. August monthly gross.

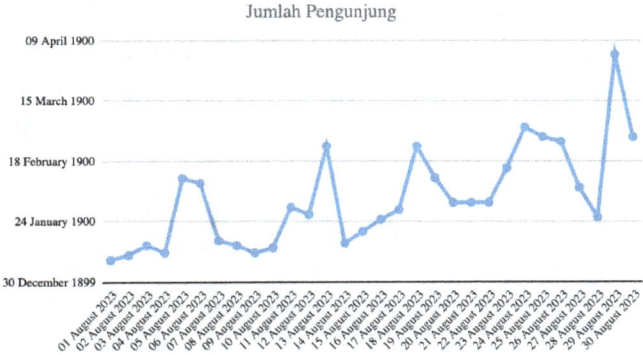

Figure 39. August monthly customers.

Table 23. Example of monthly non-cash revenue report.

DATE	E-WALLET		EDC BANK		DELIVERY		TOTAL	ACTUAL	DEDUCTION
	QRIS	SHOPEE	BCA	BNI	GOFOOD	GRABFOOD			
01 August 2023	55,000	43,000		167,000			265,000		
02 August 2023	197,000						197,000		
03 August 2023	299,800						299,800		
04 August 2023	446,000	128,000					574,000		
05 August 2023	919,000			122,000			1,041,000		
...	...	...	...	...	...	...	...	...	...
23 August 2023		969,600	43,500				1,013,100		
24 August 2023		940,300		10,200			950,500		
25 August 2023		1,000,000					1,000,000		
26 August 2023		1,221,200	240,000	49,000			1,510,200		
27 August 2023	40,000	763,000					803,000		

28 August 2023	49,000	146,000	24,000				**219,000**		
29 August 2023	1,668,100		338,000				**2,006,100**		
30 August 2023	409,000	376,000	24,000				**809,000**		
31 August 2023	1,208,000		123,000				**1,331,000**		
	14,191,950	**5,684,600**	**1,897,100**	**1,063,050**	–	–	**22,836,700**		

Table 24. Example of monthly sales per item for beverages.

No	Name	Quantity	Price	Total
1	Affogato	8	20,000	160,000
2	Mineral water	80	7,000	560,000
3	Americano	31	22,000	682,000
4	Avocado Float	12	30,000	360,000
...	...	...	...	...
41	Lychee Tea	109	18,000	1,962,000
42	Lemon Tea	77	17,000	1,309,000
43	Cappuccino	37	25,000	925,000
44	Chocolate	25	26,000	650,000
45	Kopi Susu Gula Aren (Brown Sugar)	69	24,000	1,656,000
Total		**999**		**23,644,000**

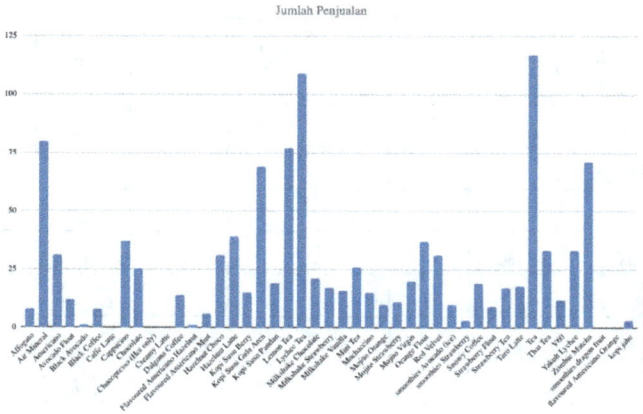

Figure 40. Graph of monthly sales per item for drinks

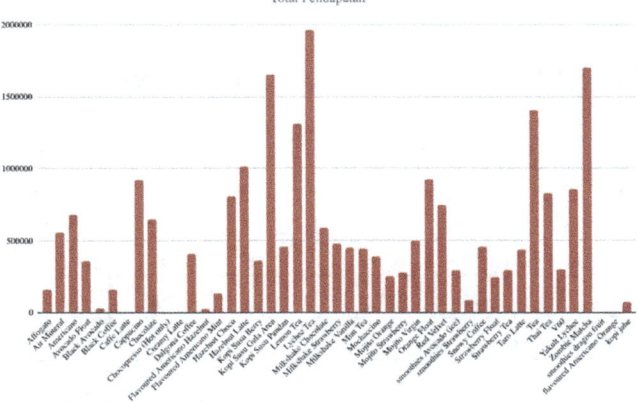

Figure 41. Graph of monthly gross revenue per item for drinks.

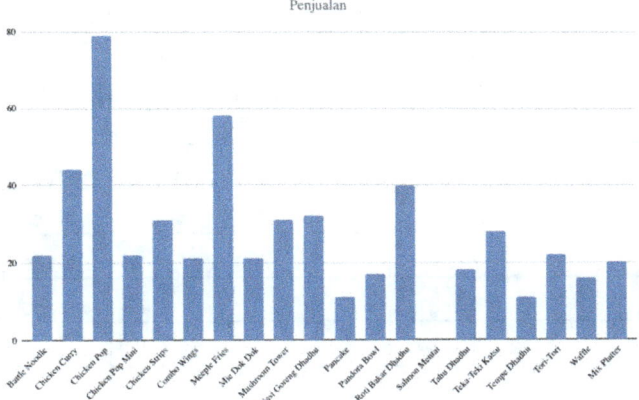

Figure 42. Graph of monthly gross revenue per item for foods.

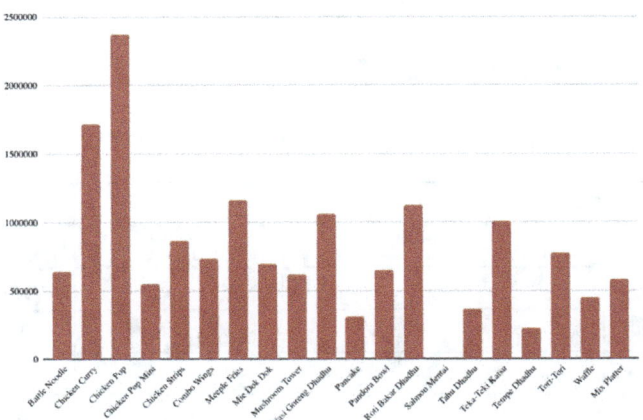

Figure 43. Graph of monthly gross revenue per item for foods.

2. EXPENSE (DAILY, WEEKLY, MONTHLY, YEARLY)

Table 25. Example of monthly expense report for August 2023.

DATE	NOTE	AMOUNT
01/08/2023	Staff meals	24,000.00
	Ice cubes x 3	24,000.00
	Ingredients	654,200.00
	Ingredients	456,000.00
	Eggs 2kg	58,000.00
	Coffee bean 2kg	260,000.00
	Coffe for v60	82,000.00
07/08/2023	Staff meals	36,000.00
	Ingredients	157,000.00
...	...	...
08/08/2023	Staff meals	24,000.00
	Insect spray	39,500.00
	Eggs 3kg	87,000.00
	Cooking oil 4L	64,000.00
	Potato 5kg	162,500.00
09/08/2023	Staff meals	12,000.00
	Ice cubes x 5	40,000.00
10/08/2023	Staff meals	36,000.00

3. BALANCE SHEET (PROFIT & LOSS)

Table 26. An example of balance sheet.

4-101	Sales F&B	37,157,000	
4-102	Sales Games	70,000	
Total Sales			**37,227,000**
5-101	COGS F&B	15,000,000	
5-102	COGS B&G	50,000	
Total COGS			**15,050,000**

Gross Profit			**22,107,000**
5-103	Electricity Expenses	3,600,000	
5-104	Salary Expenses	12,947,500	
5-105	Transportation Expenses	62,000	
5-106	Marketing Expenses	-	
5-107	Tax Expenses	445,172	
...	...	...	...
5-108	Administration Expenses	166,586	
5-109	Consumption Expenses	888,000	
5-123	Waste Management Expenses	300,000	
5-124	Discount Expenses	-	
6-101	Other income	- 1,631,800	
6-102	Other expenses	-	
Total Beban			**16,777,458**
Laba (sebelum pajak) (Profit)			**5,329,542**

4. COST OF GOODS SOLD (COGS)

Table 27. An example of cost of goods sold (COGS).

ITEM	COGS	CURRENT PRICE	PROFIT	TARGET PRICE
Combo Wings	Rp17,510	Rp35,000	100%	Rp47,277
Pop	Rp14,195	Rp30,000	111%	Rp38,327
Mie dok-dok	Rp18,296	Rp33,000	80%	Rp49,399
Fries	Rp8,563	Rp21,000	145%	Rp23,120
Mushroom	Rp7,563	Rp20,000	164%	Rp20,420
Tahu	Rp8,200	Rp20,000	144%	Rp22,140
Black Avocado	Rp16,200	Rp30,000	85%	Rp43,740
Capucino/ Café late	Rp9,200	Rp25,000	172%	Rp24,840
Mocacino	Rp11,600	Rp26,000	124%	Rp31,320
Strawberry smoothies	Rp12,900	Rp29,000	125%	Rp34,830

Zombie matcha	Rp9,150	Rp23,000	151%	Rp24,705
Hazzlenut choco	Rp11,800	Rp26,000	120%	Rp31,860

5. ATTENDANCE RECAP

Table 28. Report of staff attendance summary.

NO	ID	NAME	DIVISION	1 S	2 M	3 T	4 W	5 T	…	27 F	28 S	29 S	30 M	31 T	ON TIME	SICK	LEAVE	OFF	LATE
1	D01	Ardiawan Bagus Harisa	Creative Director						…						0	0	0	0	0
2	FT09	Sulthan Faiz	Game Master	off	t	t	h	t	…	h	t	off	h	h	15	0	0	5	11
3	FT16	Hamim	Kitchen	h	h	off	h	h	…	off	h	h	h	off	25	0	0	5	1
4	FT18	Lintang Bagus	Bar	h	h	h	h	h	…	h	off	t	s	t	20	1	0	4	6
5	PT02	Risa	SPV	h	t	h	off	i	…	h	h	h	h	t	21	0	2	3	5
6	PT04	Purwanti	Part Timer					h	…						3	0	0	0	0

6. PAYROLL SIMULATION

Table 29. Payroll simulation.

ID	NAME	DIVISION	PRESENCE					BASE SALARY	ADDITIONALS			TOTAL SALARY
			ON	SICK	LEAVE	ALPHA	OFF		DEDUCTION	INCENTIVE	DAILY INCENTIVE	
D01	Ardiawan Bagus Harisa	Direktur Kreatif						1,000,000				1,000,000
FT09	Sulthan Faiz	Game Master	26		0		5	2,500,000	119,200		24,000	2,404,800
FT16	Hamim	Kitchen	26		0		5	1,900,000	66,200	750,000	36,000	2,619,800
FT18	Lintang Bagus	Bar	26		0		4	1,800,000	46,200		24,000	1,777,800
S001	Pak Yadi	Satpam	31		0		0	1,380,000				1,380,000
S003	Pak Paino	Satpam	31	1	0		0	1,300,000				1,300,000
PT02	Risa	SPV	26		2		3	2,430,000	31,200		24000	2,422,800
PT04	Purwanti	Part Timer	3		0		0	50,000				150,000
									Total	108000		**13,055,200**

7. PAYROLL SLIP & RECEIPT OF COLLECTION

Table 30. Employee payment slip.

	Staff Payment Slip			ID	:	FT18
	Dhadhu Board Game Café					
Name	: Lintang Bagus			Date	:	01 September 2023
Division	: Bar					
Presence		Salary		Misc		
On	: 26	Base	: 1,800,000			
Sick	:			Incentive	:	24,000
Leave	: 0			Deduction	:	46,200
Off	: 4					
Late :	: 6		Total Salary :			1,777,800

Table 31. Employee payment slip.

Receipt of Salary Payment Collection			
ID	NAME	DIVISION	SIGNATURE
D01	Ardiawan Bagus Harisa	Creative Director	
FT09	Sulthan Faiz	Game Master	
PT02	Risa	Finance & Kitchen	
FT16	Hamim	Kitchen	
FT17	Lintang Bagus	Bar	
PT04	elita	Part Timer	
PT8	Purwanti	Part Timer	

B. MARKETING DOCUMENT TEMPLATES

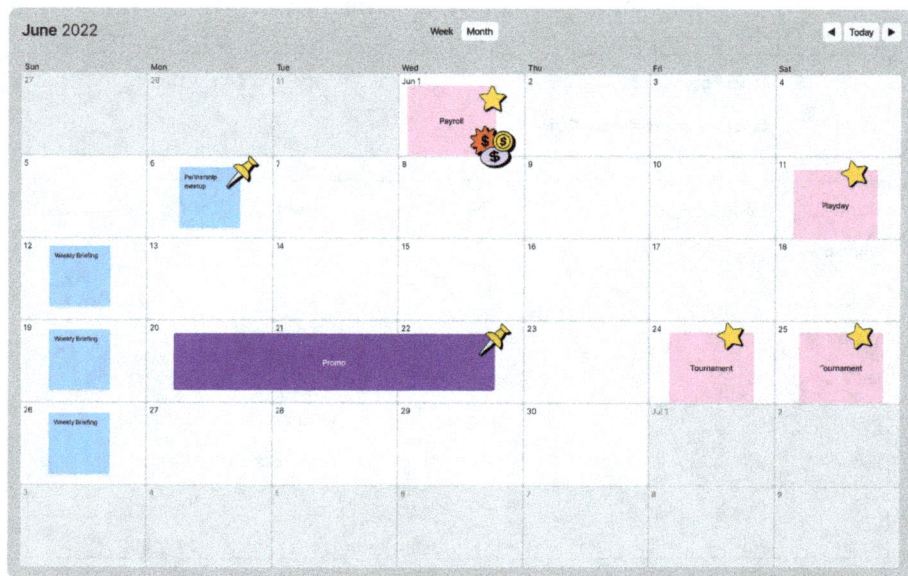

Figure 44. Event Calendar template.

Figure 45. Content Editorial Plan template.

Figure 46. Social Media Content Layout template. Left: menu; right: experience.

Figure 47. Signage template.

Table 32. Proposal template.

2020
The Art of Playing
Board Game

PROPOSAL KERJASAMA

DHADHU BOARD GAME CAFE

Jl. Timoho Raya kav. 25-26 Bulusan Tembalang
Semarang, Jawa Tengah 50722
0831 0358 9080
dhadhucafe@gmail.com

dhadhucafe_id

Daftar Isi

We don't stop playing because we grow old;
we grow old because we stop playing.

- George Bernard Shaw -

01

DHADHU BOARD GAME CAFE

Kami adalah board game cafe satu-satunya di Semarang. Dhadhu board game cafe adalah sebuah usaha dibidang *Food and Beverage* yang memiliki ciri khas board game dalam media interaksi dengan costumer. Board game sangat ditonjolkan karena selain untuk hiburan terdapat manfaat yang sangat penting bagi perkembangan individu ataupun kerjasama tim.

Dalam proposal ini kami akan membagikan informasi tentang manfaat dari board game yang mampu membuat value dari individu maupun tim meningkat.

02

QUEST

Perkembangan individu adalah hal esensial yang wajib dipertimbangkan untuk kerja sama tim. Berkembangnya teknologi membuat lingkungan kerja yang dulunya kompetitif berubah menjadi tempat kerja di mana kolaborasi dan kerja sama antar individu dapat menghasilkan kesuksesan.

Dengan memberikan perhatian kepada individu akan dapat mendorong pengembangan keterampilan dan kolaborasi yang sangat berpengaruh terhadap kinerja tim. Metode kolaborasi dapat memaksimalkan kemampuan kerja sama anggota tim. Denagan saling berkomunikasi dan memahami perasaan maka akan memunculkan solusi cerdas untuk tim.

MISSION

Dhadhu board game cafe terdorong untuk melakukan inovasi. Pendekatan secara langsung menggunakan media board game. Board game sendiri adalah sebuah permainan yang telah didesain sedemikian rupa dalam bentuk fisik yang membuat para pemainya akan lebih sering berinteraksi. Kami akan membawa anda merasakan secara langsung keajaiban board game.

Rewards

Entertainment	: Penyeimbang pekerjaan dan kebutuhan personal
Game-Based Learning	: Pembelajaran yang lebih atraktif dan menyenangkan
Branding & Marketing	: Menaikkan *brand awareness* menggunakan game.

ENTERTAINMENT

Hiburan dapat digunakan sebagai penyeimbang antara pekerjaan dan kebutuhan personal seperti kesehatan mental dan fisik individu. Dimana hal tersebut dapat berpengaruh pada kinerja.

Bermain board game akan membuat pikiran anda menjadi lebih *fresh*, karena pikiran anda akan teralih dari faktor-faktor penyebab stres. Berinteraksi dan bercanda dengan sesama rekan bisa menjadi stress reliever tersendiri. Pikiran anda akan menjadi rileks karena aktivitas tertawa.

ICE BREAKING

Suasana tim yang positif akan meruntuhkan penghalang sosial antar team. Selain itu individu akan lebih rileks ketika berada dalam lingkungan kerja. Kami akan membuat suasana Ice Breaking menjadi lebih atraktif dan menyenangkan dengan menggunakan board game.

GAME-BASED LEARNING

Dengan menggunakan board game, kami membuat suasana pembelajaran lebih atraktif dan menyenangkan. Kita dapat memberikan stimulus pada tiga bagian penting dalam pembelajaran yaitu *emotional, intellectual, psycomotoric*. individu akan lebih interaktif karena dapat terjun secara langsung ke dalam pembelajaran dan dapat meninggalkan kesan yang positif.

TRAINING

Individu yang memiliki karakter akan lebih siap untuk menghadapi tantangan saat bekerja dan mampu mempelajari kesalahan.

Lingkungan tim yang kompak dan membangun dapat membentuk talenta individu mengembangkan potensinya. Training menggunakan team bonding dapat menjadi strategi manajemen untuk menciptakan usaha agar tim menjadi solid dan kompak.

WORKSHOP

Setiap individu memiliki kejenuhan dalam profesi yang di jalani saat ini. Untuk mendapatkan tambahan kualifikasi profesi yang baru. Kami akan menumbuhkan minat anda dari skill baru yang didapat dari board game

SEMINAR

Pembaharuan pengetahuan dan keterampilan sangat dibutuhkan oleh setiap individu di lingkungan kompetitif. Kami memiliki metode kreatif, dengan mengajak anda memperbaharui talenta anda hanya dengan bermain board game. Kami berharap dapat membantu anda dalam menumbuhkan jiwa individu *"passionate talent"*.

BRANDING & MARKETING

Bayangkan ketika *client* atau *partner* anda menggunakan produk dan/atau jasa anda seperti mereka bermain game. Tanpa sadar dan menyenangkan.

Gamification! Kita dapat menggunakan mekanisme *gaming* diluar kegiatan bermain game untuk mencapai tujuan. Strategi menaikkan *brand awarness* dapat disampaikan dengan board game.

07

08

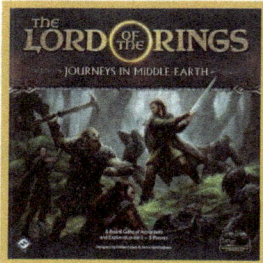

MAGICAL SPELL

"It is simply magical. It is a board game."
Jadi mari kita gunakan keajaiban board game untuk berbagi inovasi kreatif dan mengembangkan potensi.

IT'S TIME
FOR YOU

Dengan penjelasan manfaat bermain board game untuk pengembangan potensi tim dan individu diatas, kami berharap dapat menjalin kerjasama dengan instansi anda. Tertantangkah anda mencoba secara langsung keajaiban board game?

09

10

ICE BREAKING

Game Rental — ~~55k~~ 30-50k/ game

Rent our game for 1 day 3 days now so you can enjoy your chilling time.
You may find our game catalogue.

Game Master — 100k/ GM

Learn by doing to level up your skills of solution design, teamwork, team bonding, team evaluation, or special case.

Free Ice breaking bundle — FREE!

You can get free of charge ice breaking by buying our takeaway menu with minimum payment of 150k. We will send them right away!

Bahagia adalah salah satu kebutuhan yang wajib kita penuhi.
Ajak keluarga dan relasimu untuk bersuka cita bersama-sama!

BRANDING & MARKETNG

Gamification System — 25m* bundle (save 10m)

Deliver your product's or service's value and deepen your customer engagement within social media or any marketing tools.
- R&D 18m
- 3 month training 9m
- 3 weekly & monthly events 5m*

Game as media — 75m* bundle (save 10m*)

Make your customer discover the intangible values of your product or service by letting them to have fun by custom game.
- R&D and Game Design 26m
- Production guide 5jt
- Training 5m
- 1 weekly & monthly events 5m*
- Game productions 50-80m*

Board game Balap Kuliner

Bayangkan jika customer anda belum tidak sadar telah menggunakan value anda. Dalam jangka pendek, gamifikasi akan berlangsung menjadi aksi yang memberikan edukasi terhadap produk dan jasa anda. Customer journey membangun value lebih jadi yang sangat brilian!

Workshop

Seminar — 100k/ pax or 750k bundle

Learn from the best creator with the topic of game, game-based learning and gamification.

Workshop — 50k/pax or 1.5m bundle

Learn by doing to level up your skills of solution design, teamwork, team bonding, team evaluation, or special case.

Team Training — 15m/sessions or 25m bundle

Train your team to get the optimal efforts to produce the best work.
We have hadled various team from any topic domains.

Ayo naik level dan belajar dalam lingkungan yang positif sehingga dapat menunjang karir dan karakter kamu!

OUR CLIENTS

 wivi indonesia

We understand you have questions. Please contact us at
whatsapp +62 812 / 8464 055 or email dhadhucafe@gmail.com
(Dhadhu Cafe, Jl. xinum Sengrapto Km. 76-18 Bulusan, Tembalang, Semarang)

When playing a game,
the goal is to win.
But it is the goal that's is important,
not the winning.

- Reiner Knizia -

#ngerollyuk

C. PRODUCTION DOCUMENT TEMPLATES

Table 33. Template of stock in, out, and wasted ingredients.

Item	Unit	Date								Total
		...	17	18	19	20	21	...	31	
In		...						...		-
Ades Mineral	pcs	...		48.00				...	48.00	96.00
Alpukat	gr	...					1,500.00	...		4,500.00
Chocolatos Coklat	gr	...						...		1,000.00
Out		...						...		-
Ades	pcs	...	2.00	6.00	5.00	3.00	4.00	...	4.00	80.00
Alpukat	gr	...	300.00	400.00	1,000.00		500.00	...		4,500.00
Chocolatos Coklat	gr	...						...		1,500.00
Wasted		...						...		-
Alpukat	gr	...						...	400	400

Table 34. Template of stocktaking.

No	Item	Initial	Final	Total Entry	Out	Unit	Price	Total Initial	Total Out	Total Final
1	Ades	47	96.00	80.00	63.0	pcs	2,500.00	117,500	157,500	240,000
2	Alpukat	0	4,500.00	4,500.00	-	gr	30.00	-	-	135,000
3	Buah Naga	0	-	-	-	gr	80.00	-	-	-
...	...	...	...	...	...	...	...	...	...	...
18	Jahe	14	-	2.00	12.0	pcs	1,000.00	14,000	12,000	-
19	Jeruk Lemon	500	2,000.00	2,000.00	500.0	gr	20.00	10,000	10,000	40,000
20	Jeruk Nipis	500	2,500.00	2,500.00	500.0	gr	15.00	7,500	7,500	37,500
21	Kopi Arabica	0	-	-	-	gr		-	-	-
22	Kopi Espresso	0	6,000.00	5,000.00	1,000.0	gr	130.00	-	130,000	780,000
23	Kopi V60	245	15.00	195.00	65.0	gr	260.00	63,700	16,900	3,900
24	Leci Kaleng	2	17.00	17.00	2.0	kaleng	33,600.00	67,200	67,200	571,200
								4,661,852	2,836,215	7,774,090

Table 35. Template of stock summary.

Table of Stocktaking – August 2023			
Kitchen		**Bar**	
Initial	7,923,820	Initial	4,661,852
Purchase		Purchase	
Out	12,543,450	Out	2,836,215
Final	6,145,670	Final	7,774,090
Wasted	10%	Wasted	3%
COGS			
Remaining ingredients			**13,919,760**

Table 36. Template of daily expense for bar, kitchen, and office.

No	Item	Date										Total
		...	17	18	19	20	21	22	29	30	31	
1	Ades	...		118,000			118,000				118,000	354,000
2	Alpukat	...					45,000					150,000
...	...	...	...	...	...	...	...	...	...	...	...	...
6	Chocolatos Coklat	...										130,000
7	Chocolatos Matcha	...						36,000	36,000			72,000
10	Es Batu	...	16,000		24,000		24,000				40,000	256,000
11	Es Krim Coklat	...						174,000				588,000
12	Es Krim Strawberry	...						174,000				588,000
13	Es Krim Vanilla	...						522,000				1,350,000
14	Fresh Milk	...										-
15	Gula Pasir	...			67,500		14,000					291,500
16	Jahe	...										-
TOTAL		...	226,000	228,800	315,800	71,000	441,000	948,000	361,000	25,000	829,500	12,478,776

Table 37. Template of employee daily consumption expense.

Employee Daily Consumption Incentive			
Period:		**Aug-23**	
Date	**Qt**	**Amount**	**Balance**
01 August 2023	2	24,000	24,000

02 August 2023	3	36,000	60,000
03 August 2023	2	24,000	84,000
04 August 2023	3	36,000	120,000
05 August 2023	2	24,000	144,000
06 August 2023	2	24,000	168,000
07 August 2023	3	36,000	204,000
08 August 2023	2	24,000	228,000
09 August 2023	1	12,000	240,000
10 August 2023	3	36,000	276,000
11 August 2023	2	24,000	300,000
12 August 2023	4	48,000	348,000
Total		912,000	14,712,000

Table 38. Template of summary of daily expense for bar, kitchen, and office.

NOTE	AMOUNT
BEVERAGE	12,478,776
FOOD	8,911,659
F&B EXPENSE	**21,390,435**
MATERIAL	6,689,900
CONSUMPTION	912,000
TOTAL BELANJA	**28,992,335**

D. GAME MASTER DOCUMENT TEMPLATES

Table 39. Template of consignment games.

No	Game	Supplier	Initial Stock	Sales 2021	Sales 2022	Paid Stock	Unpaid Stock	COGS	Unpaid
1	Laga Jakarta	Chiveus	14	3	7	10	0	200000	0
2	Unmask	Chiveus	3	1	1	2	0	156000	0
3	Jalan-Jalan	Chiveus	9	1	1	2	0	110000	0
4	Cenayang	Memento Craft	9	9	0	9	0	90000	0

5	Balap Kuliner	Kompas	5	4	1	5	0	259000	0
6	Amabua	beakbug	10	4	6	10	0	105000	0
7	Flipeek	Coralis Ent	4	3	0	3	0	200000	0
8	Soocer17	Jack Darwid	6	0	0	0	0	150000	0
9	zamzamy	sebangku	9	4	0	0	4	100000	400000
10	CATAN 1995	-	3	1	0	1	0	0	0
11	Match Cat	Hompimpa Games	14	5	9	14	0	85000	0
12	Veggie Colors	Hompimpa Games	14	1	8	9	0	85000	0
							Total		400000

Table 40. Template of currently being maintained or rotated game.

Games that need to be rotated			
Nama	Category	Damage	Price
Dixit	Light	Sleeve, Player's voting card	
Catan classic	Medium Light	Component lost	
Alchemist	Heavy	Never played	Rp. 680.000
Cash & Guns	Light	Box Tear	
Santorini	Light	Box Tear	
Gogo Gelato	Light	Box tear	
Imagineers	Heavy	Never played	
Quoridor	light	Box tear, component lost	

Table 41. Template of List of Games Available to Rent.

No	Game	Link to Description	Category	Rent per Day	Status
1	7 wonders Duel	https://boardgamegeek.com/boardgame/173346/7-wonders-duel	Light	Rp30,000.00	
2	Alchemists	https://boardgamegeek.com/boardgame/161970/alchemists	Heavy	Rp55,000.00	Available
3	Batman: Gotham city strategy game	https://boardgamegeek.com/boardgame/130911/batman-gotham-city-strategy-game	Heavy	Rp55,000.00	Available
4	Blood Rage	https://boardgamegeek.com/boardgame/170216/blood-rage	Heavy	Rp55,000.00	Available
...	...	...	...	...	...

11	BRASS	https://boardgamegeek.com/boardgame/28720/brass-lancashire	Heavy	Rp55,000.00	Available
12	Cacao	https://boardgamegeek.com/boardgame/171499/cacao	Light	Rp30,000.00	
13	Cash & Gun	https://boardgamegeek.com/boardgame/155362/cah-n-guns-second-edition	Light	Rp30,000.00	available
14	CATAN (1995)	https://boardgamegeek.com/boardgame/13/catan	Medium	Rp40,000.00	Available
15	Catan Family	https://boardgamegeek.com/boardgame/147240/catan-family-edition	Medium	Rp40,000.00	

E. MANAGEMENT DOCUMENT TEMPLATES

Table 42. Template of letter.

 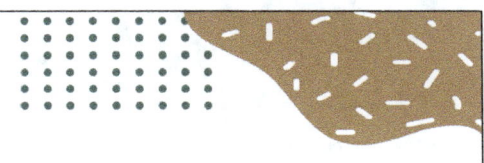

Letter of ‹fill›

NUMBER: D001/HRD/I/2021

The undersigned:

  Name   : Ardiawan Bagus Harisa

  Position   : Creative Director

  Address   : Central Java

Hereby certify that:

  Name   : Antoni Feri Saputra

  Position   : Cook Helper

  Address   : Karang Panas, Semarang

Is an employee of Dhadhu Board Game Café who has been working since December 27, 2019, until January 31, 2021. Throughout their employment, they have demonstrated dedication and loyalty to the company.

This certificate is hereby issued for the intended purpose.

Semarang, January 31, 2021

Ardiawan Bagus Harisa
Creative Director

Table 43. Template of warning letter.

Warning Letter
NUMBER: D001/HRD/I/2021

This Warning Letter is issued by the company and addressed to:

Name   : Sultan Faiz Ardiansyah

Position   : Game Master

This warning letter is issued based on the repeated mistakes you have made and have been repeatedly warned about. As an employee, it is expected that you behave professionally by adhering to the company's rules and regulations. This includes: abusing authority and taking time off outside the Café.

Therefore, the company will issue the first warning letter. This is intended to provide guidance and warning to you to comply with the company's rules and regulations and to refrain from making further mistakes that could harm the company.

Thus, this warning letter is issued for your attention and compliance.

Semarang, 12 June 2022

Staff   Creative Director

Sultan Faiz Ardiansyah   Ardiawan Bagus Harisa

Table 44. Template of monthly report & evaluation.

November
Montly Evaluation

Inshight Instagram

Expense

Summary:
Presentase Cost:
- HPP Oktober : 22%
- Gaji Karyawan : 44%
- Laba : 18%
- Operasional : 16%

	Periode November 2021		
4-101	Penjualan F&B	25.096.000	
4-102	Penjualan B&G	245.000	
	Total Penjualan		25.341.000
5-101	HPP F&B	5.588.954	
5-102	HPP B&G	-	
	Total HPP		5.588.954
	Laba Kotor		19.752.046
5-103	Beban Listrik, Wifi & Telp.	-	
5-104	Beban Gaji	11.067.000	
5-105	Beban Transport	-	
5-106	Beban Pemasaran	150.000	
5-107	Beban Pajak	1.595.688	
5-108	Beban Administrasi	176.801	
5-109	Beban Konsumsi	684.000	
5-120	Beban Perlengkapan	449.750	
5-121	Beban Pest Control	-	
5-122	Beban Maintenance	-	
5-123	Beban Sampah	300.000	
5-124	Beban Diskon	-	
6-101	Pendapatan Lain-lain	-	
6-102	Beban Lain-lain	738.000	
	Total Beban		15.161.239
	Laba Bersih Sebelum Pajak		4.590.806

Profit

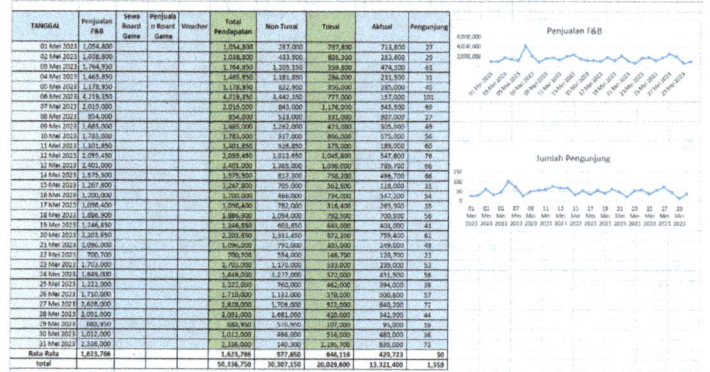

Progress within 2 months (August - September)

Bulan	Omset		Rata-Rata Penjualan	Pengunjung
Agustus	Rp	22.938.650	Rp 917.546	672
September	Rp	28.768.000	Rp 1.106.462	767
Oktober	Rp	34.261.000	Rp 1.317.731	876
November	Rp	25.341.000	Rp 1.013.640	748

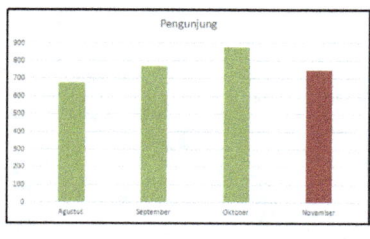

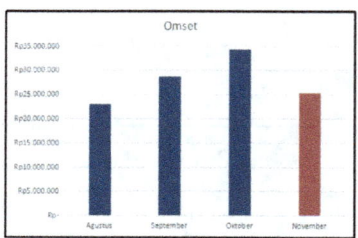

Kalender Aktivitas Mei

Kegiatan yang sudah dilakukan di bulan Mei:

- Sulthan melakukan gath card game yu gi-oh dll di Dhadhu setiap hari sabtu dan minggu jam 11 siang
- Membeli botol kaca dan plastic untuk coldbrew
- Melakukan briefing management secara internal selama 2 hr
- Melakukan briefing mingguan
- Melakukan promo bulanan yaitu setiap pembelian main course free ice tea
- Merubah harga HPP dan harga jual
- Menambahkan menu baru (Coldbrew dan mix platter)

Yu Gi-Oh!

One Piece

Table 45. Template annual report & evaluation.

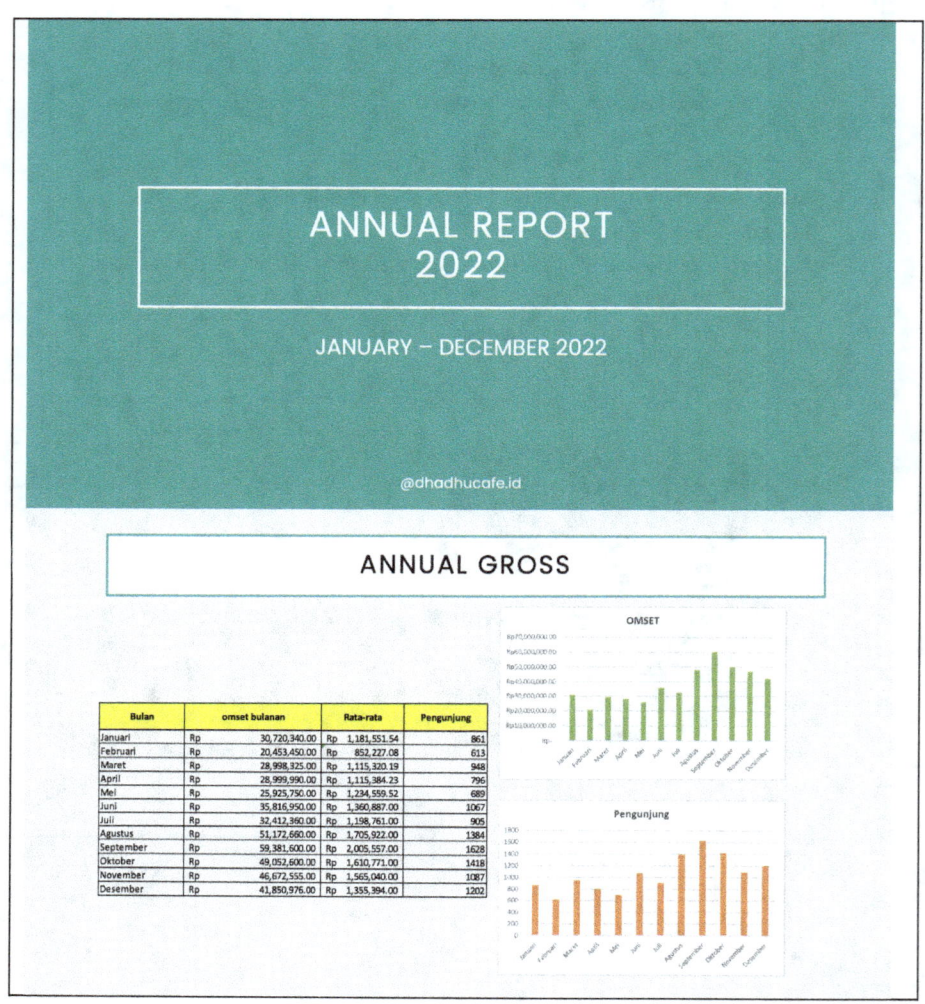

2020

Bulan	Omset	Pengeluaran
Januari	Rp -	Rp 22,883,416.00
Februari	Rp 76,063,800.00	Rp 65,282,741.00
Maret	Rp 2,390,550.00	
April	Rp -	Rp -
Mei	Rp 1,425,500.00	Rp 710,500.00
Juni	Rp 24,798,870.00	Rp 25,277,594.00
Juli	Rp 41,827,500.00	Rp 45,986,997.00
Agustus	Rp 52,675,500.00	Rp 54,978,671.00
September	Rp 61,999,950.00	Rp 65,754,555.00
Oktober	Rp 70,222,050.00	Rp 60,976,876.00
November	Rp 58,970,000.00	Rp 45,393,389.00
Desember	Rp 51,132,300.00	Rp 52,005,278.00
Total	Rp 441,506,020.00	Rp 439,250,017.00

2021

Bulan	Omset	Pengeluaran
Januari	Rp42,512,250	Rp43,543,438
Februari	Rp30,610,250	Rp32,557,297
Maret	Rp46,061,000	Rp40,210,153
April	Rp34,164,250	Rp34,261,079
Mei	Rp33,646,000	Rp35,700,720
Juni	Rp26,499,000	Rp28,236,313
Juli	Rp1,107,000	Rp7,880,628
Agustus	Rp24,854,350	Rp23,091,903
September	Rp28,841,000	Rp25,444,013
Oktober	Rp34,871,000	Rp29,444,331
November	Rp25,341,000	Rp18,562,194
Desember	Progress	Progress
Total	Rp328,507,400	Rp318,932,070

2022

No	Bulan	omset bulanan	pengeluaran
1	Januari	Rp 30,720,340.00	Rp 23,687,882.00
2	Februari	Rp 20,453,450.00	Rp 28,521,724.00
3	Maret	Rp 28,998,325.00	Rp 24,061,302.00
4	April	Rp 28,999,990.00	Rp 29,285,739.00
5	Mei	Rp 25,925,750.00	Rp 31,053,476.00
6	Juni	Rp 35,816,950.00	Rp 29,396,131.00
7	Juli	Rp 32,412,360.00	Rp 24,662,160.00
8	Agustus	Rp 51,172,660.00	Rp 38,250,367.00
9	September	Rp 59,381,600.00	Rp 46,525,678.00
10	Oktober	Rp 49,052,600.00	Rp 40,964,311.00
11	November	Rp 46,672,555.00	Rp 37,874,186.00
12	Desember	Rp 41,850,976.00	Rp 32,794,173.00
	Total	Rp451,457,556.00	Rp 387,077,129.00

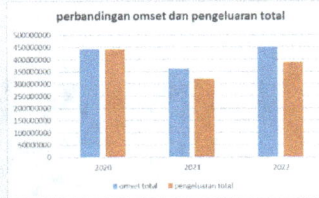

perbandingan omset dan pengeluaran total

Sales Summary

577	387	534	1198
Fries	Curry	Matcha	Tea

MENU SALES

Makanan

No	Nama Makanan	Jumlah
1	Meeple Fries	577
2	Chicken Curry	387
3	Nasi Goreng Dhadhu	309
4	Roti Bakar Dhadhu	309
5	Chicken Strips	277
6	Salmon Mentai	265
7	Mie Dok Dok	256
8	Chicken Pop	236
9	Waffle	228
10	Tahu Dhadhu	211
11	Mushroom Tower	208
12	Tori-Tori	208
13	Teka-Teki Katsu	204
14	Tempe Dhadhu	188
15	Chicken Pop Mini	179
16	Combo Wings	146
17	Pancake	138
18	Pandora Bowl	126
19	Battle Noodle	77
20	Chicken Creamy Soup	50
21	tomyum	13
22	udang mentai	6
22	batagore	2

batagore — sampai juni
udang mentai — sampai juli
tom yum — juni-juli
cream soup — dari juni

Minuman

No	Nama Minuman	Jumlah
1	Tea	1198
2	Air Mineral	781
3	Zombie Matcha	534
4	Chocolate	512
5	Lychee Tea	480
6	Kopi Susu Gula Aren	473
7	Yakult Lychee	437
8	Red Velvet	402
9	Hazelnut Latte	388
10	Hazelnut Choco	371
11	Thai Tea	337
12	Caffe Latte	266
13	Americano	257
14	Creamy Latte	240
15	Cappucino	215
16	Milkshake Chocolate	201
17	Milkshake Vanilla	197
18	Lemon Tea	187
19	Mojito Strawberry	184
20	Taro Latte	179
21	Milkshake Strawberry	155
22	Strawberry Tea	143
23	Avocado Float	140
24	Mint Tea	132
25	Snowy Coffee	124
26	Kopi Susu Pandan	118
27	Mojito Virgin	111
28	Mojito Orange	96
29	Strawberry Float	94
30	Affogato	91
31	smoothies Strawberry	87
32	Dalgona Coffee	85
33	smoothies Avocado (ice)	80
34	Mochaccino	75
35	Kopi Susu Berry	74
36	V60	61
37	Flavoured Americano Hazelnut	51
38	Black Coffee	44
39	Orange Float	36
40	Black Avocado	25
41	Flavoured Americano Mint	25
42	flavoured Americano Orange	16
43	kopi jahe	9
44	Chocopresso (Hot only)	5
45	smoothies dragon fruit	5

dragon fruits juni-sept
americano orange baru ada juli

ACTIVITY CALENDAR – DECEMBER

Pengadaan Game

Roll dice event nataru

STB dan Stand TV

Perbaikan saluran pembuangan di dapur

Sinar UV untuk pengecheckan uang

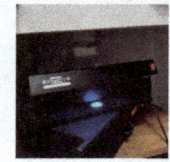

NOBAR FINAL WORLD CUP 2022

2023 AGENDA

- Aktif APIBGI
- Update menu
- Update game
- Efisiensi Q1-Q2
- Target dividen +100%
- Pengolahan space kosong
- Kontrak, THR, Share
- Sertifikasi HALAL

SOCMED INSIGHT

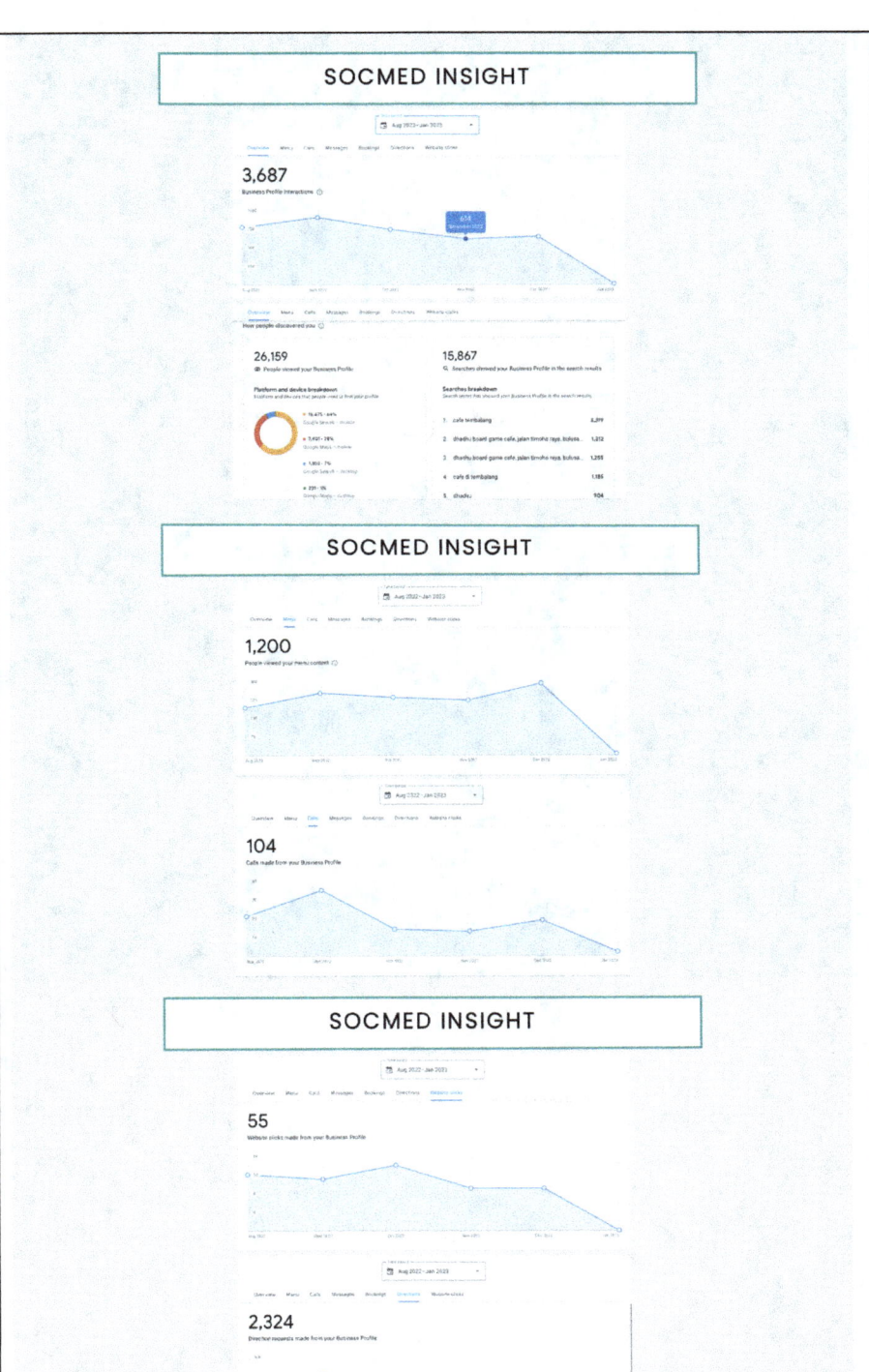

SOCMED INSIGHT

SOCMED INSIGHT

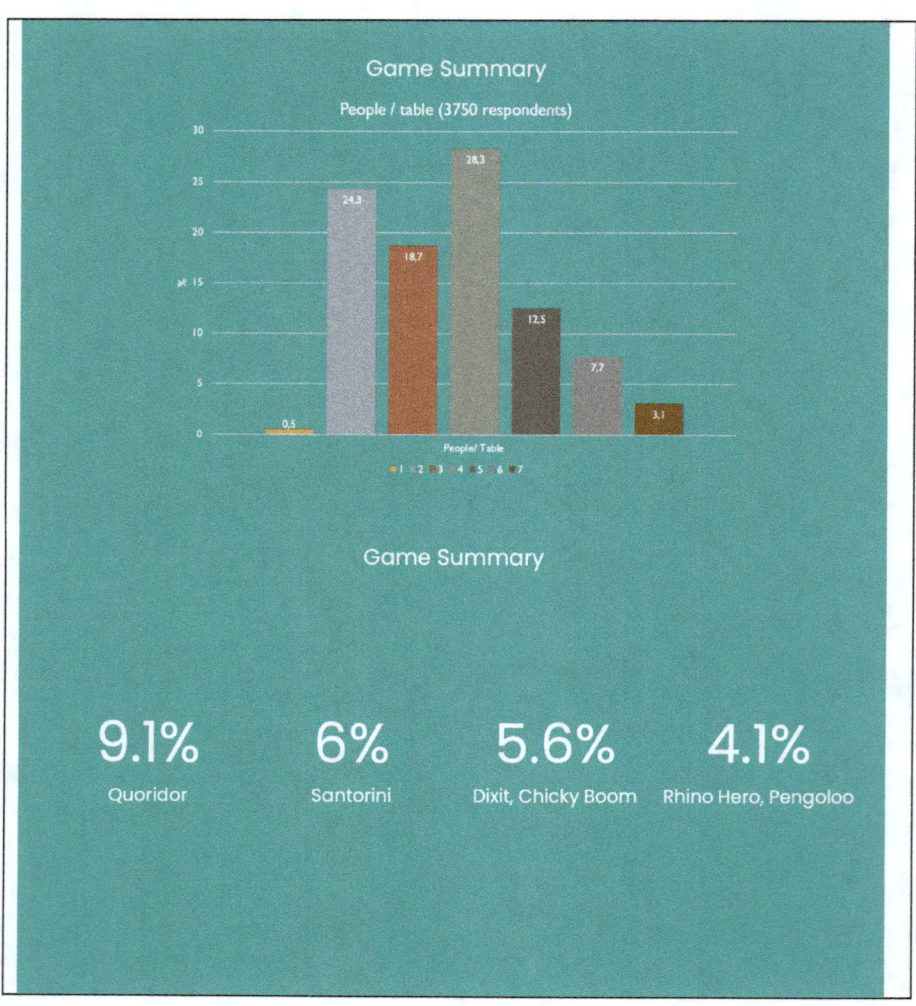

Game Summary

People / table (3750 respondents)

People/ Table
■ 1 ■ 2 ■ 3 ■ 4 ■ 5 ■ 6 ■ 7

Game Summary

9.1%	6%	5.6%	4.1%
Quoridor	Santorini	Dixit, Chicky Boom	Rhino Hero, Pengoloo

Game Summary

Game Master

Sultan · Sandi · Fino · Xeni · Dimas · Bagus · Wicak · Other

Thank you.
#ngerollyuk in 2023!

@dhadhucafe.id

X. DEVELOPMENT

A. STAFF DEVELOPMENT

Some things we can do for staff development:

1. **Reading Books**: Once a month, select 1 book related to appropriate material and interesting for the staff according to their divisions. Force them to share during each monthly briefing so that all staff can learn various things in a short time. In addition to books, we can also use management articles from the internet.

2. **Training**: All staff, both part-time and full-time, should ideally be given training directly from management. Avoid asking other staff to provide initial training, as staff have different performance standards. To minimize substandard work quality under management standards, new staff should be given direct training from management from the beginning and must be firm. Then, for full-time staff who can work for a long period, periodic training should be given. For example, for staff who have been working for more than 1 year, provide training according to their field of work so that they can advance to a higher level. Then, every few years, provide training.

3. **Breaks & Team Bonding**: Once a year, breaks should be held, and at the same time, use that time for team bonding. For this, you in management must have special planning and savings for team bonding. For example, budget for meals for a number of staff, and also for gaming activities and equipment. It might take around Rp. 2,000,000 for about 10 people.

B. BUSINESS DEVELOPMENT

Here are some essential things for business development:

1. **Collection Updates (Casual & Medium)**: Every 1-3 months, buy new games to update the collection, especially for casual and medium titles. Because the majority of players in board game Cafés are dominated by casual and medium gamers.

2. **F&B Menu Updates**: Every 3 months, or 1 quarter, evaluate the menu. If there are menus that have been less popular for several quarters, try to push selling. Ask frontline staff to push so that the menu can be sold

more. If the menu is still difficult to sell, consider replacing it with other trending menus.

3. **Maintain Social Media**: Update your business's social media at least once a week. Let customers know about your business's existence. Also, use other marketing models such as LinkedIn or even word of mouth, and sponsorship.

4. **Membership & Loyalty Program**: Make your customers part of your community inclusively. For example, when determining new collections for games to be added, try voting or asking for opinions from your customers. In addition, members also receive special discounts. Thus, making them more appreciated.

5. **Community & Collaboration Events**: Conduct an event at least once every 1-2 months. It doesn't have to be with the board game community. You might be able to invite other communities such as bloggers, book reading, role-playing (DnD), and others.

6. **B2B & Reservations**: Massive private reservations greatly help the sustainability of a restaurant. A private reservation worth more than Rp. 5,000,000 can certainly help provide safety for income. Therefore, try to have private reservations every month.

7. **Sustainable Management**: A business can be considered successful if it exceeds the initial capital and can run without any intervention from the owner or directors. Organize management along with all available resources. So, you must ensure that all processes can run according to the task delegation given to staff from each division.

***

FINAL WORDS

That's it, folks. You have learned about the profile of a board game café, the business model of a board game café, examples of company rules, and SOPs. You have also been provided with examples of checklists, working employment contracts, and how to evaluate your staff. We have also included menu photos and recipes, various document templates you might need, and finally, a tip on how to develop your board game café. We know this book does not cover all the materials you may have wanted, because mature knowledge is obtained through direct learning as you manage the actual café. However, with the limited information in this book, you gain fundamental knowledge on how to run a board game café yourself.

REFERENCES

Baehr, E., & Loomis, E. (2015). *Get Backed: Craft Your Story, Build the Perfect Pitch Deck, and Launch the Venture of Your Dreams*. Harvard Business Review Press.

Borchard, A., Schwappach, D. L. B., Barbir, A., & Bezzola, P. (2012). A Systematic Review of the Effectiveness, Compliance, and Critical Factors for Implementation of Safety Checklists in Surgery. *Annals of Surgery, 256*(6), 925–933. https://doi.org/10.1097/SLA.0b013e3182682f27

Degani, A., & Wiener, E. L. (1991). *Human factors of flight-deck checklists: The normal checklist* (NAS 1.26:177549). https://ntrs.nasa.gov/citations/19910017830

Donovan, T. (2018). *It's all a game: A short history of board games*. ATLANTIC Books.

Gurhananda, I., & Wandebori, H. (n.d.). STRATEGIC MARKETING FOR RESTAURANT BUSINESS (CASE STUDY OF LAWANGWANG CAFÉ). *Journal of Business and Management*.

Harisa, A. B. (2020, February 16). *Dhadhu Board Game Cafe*. https://dhadhu-board-game-cafe.business.site

Hou, C.-I. (2013). Study On Decision-Making for Cafe Management Alternatives. *International Journal of Computer Science and Information Technology, 5*(6), 67–75. https://doi.org/10.5121/ijcsit.2013.5605

Kardasis, P., & Loucopoulos, P. (2004). Expressing and organising business rules. *Information and Software Technology, 46*(11), 701–718. https://doi.org/10.1016/j.infsof.2003.12.003

Konieczny, P. (2019). Golden Age of Tabletop Gaming: Creation of the Social Capital and Rise of Third Spaces for Tabletop Gaming in the 21st Century. *Polish Sociological Review, 206*, 199–216.

Manasa, K. V. L., & Reddy, N. (2009, September 1). *Role of Training in Improving Performance. | IUP Journal of Soft Skills | EBSCOhost*. https://openurl.ebsco.com/contentitem/gcd:47506253?sid=ebsco:plink:crawler&id=ebsco:gcd:47506253

Manghani, K. (2011). Quality assurance: Importance of systems and standard operating procedures. *Perspectives in Clinical Research, 2*(1), 34–37. https://doi.org/10.4103/2229-3485.76288

Osterwalder, A., & Pigneur, Y. (2010). *Business Model Generation: A Handbook for Visionaries, Game Changers, and Challengers*. John Wiley & Sons.

Simon, H. A. (1951). A Formal Theory of the Employment Relationship. *Econometrica, 19*(3), 293–305. https://doi.org/10.2307/1906815

BIOGRAPHY

ARDIAWAN BAGUS HARISA

Bagus is a computer science lecturer at Universitas Dian Nuswantoro. During his spare time, he directs his small software team at Pandonga Creatives. On weekends, he takes on the role of Creative Director at Dhadhu Board Game Café. He also manages GACLab (Game AI Code Lab) at Universitas Dian Nuswantoro, a game lab focusing on AI and procedural content generation. Bagus got his bachelor's degree at UDINUS in 2015, and awarded a Master of Science at National Taiwan University of Science and Technology (NTUST) in 2018. You can reach him at his website at www.harisa.id.

PULUNG NURTANTIO ANDONO

Pulung obtained his bachelor's degree in Informatics Engineering at Trisakti University in 2006 and his master's degree in Informatics Engineering at Dian Nuswantoro University in 2009. He completed his doctoral studies at the Sepuluh November Institute of Technology (ITS) in 2014. Currently, he serves as a professor in the Informatics Engineering Study Program, Faculty of Computer Science, at Universitas Dian Nuswantoro. He is also interested in entrepreneurship and manages a coffee shop called "Fotokopi".

www.ingramcontent.com/pod-product-compliance
Lightning Source LLC
Chambersburg PA
CBHW071055290526
45795CB00004B/1500